Soulfluent® Leadership Business Guide

Amplify Your *Message*, *Visibility*, and *Profits* by Leveraging Your Archetype

Priscilla Stephan

The Soulfluent® Leadership Business Guide.
Amplify Your Message, Visibility, and Profits by Leveraging Your Archetype

Soulfluent Magic Press
www.priscillastephan.com

ISBN: 978-0-578-35880-2
Library of Congress Control Number: 2022900820

Photography: Michelle Hayes Studio
Cover Design: Jessica Lynn Design

Printed in the United States

Soulfluent® Leadership Business Guide

Amplify Your *Message*, *Visibility,* and *Profits*
by Leveraging Your Archetype

"If we crave some cosmic purpose, then let us find ourselves a worthy goal."

– Carl Sagan

*Dedicated to you, the dreamer,
rule-breaker, rabble-rouser, trailblazer,
and way-shower who dares, in spite
of the odds, to create a better world
and who, in so doing, inspires us to
rise up and live our fullest potential.*

*Your courage activates our courage.
Your vision ignites ours. Your soul
emboldens our soul.*

Foreword

One of the greatest and most noble pursuits of this human journey is to identify and embody the attributes of a great "leader."

Part of the challenge of identifying the path of true leadership today is that the old conventional models are entrenched in societal systems that not only no longer serve us as an evolving collective, but are in fact relics of paradigms that are crumbling all around us.

Very real change is afoot in every aspect of our modern society as our health, political, and economic systems are all being scrutinized and in many cases dismantled. What we are being shown in the process is just how much work we have to do to rewrite our stories of what "success" is actually based upon, and from there, what true leadership for these emerging times will look like.

One thing we know for certain is that too much of our training and guidance on leadership has historically come from one very distinct demographic, a demographic that has uncoincidentally benefited greatly from the very systems that they created and perpetuated. These voices and these systems were deeply undemocratic, misogynistic, fundamentally reinforced white privilege and white supremacy, and ultimately now fail to offer guidance that will sustain us during these times of great shift, or deliver us to a more just society. We are called to envision a society which is guided by leaders focused not on extraction and consumption, but instead on repair and unity, leaders who lead for the benefit of all.

In my work over the last twenty-five years as a consultant, entrepreneur, and intuitive strategist I have been drawn to individuals who embody and model great leadership in spite of the inherent flaws in our public systems. What I've witnessed and learned along the way is not being taught in business schools or by leadership coaches because it is an entirely new way of looking at leadership, and an entirely new way of defining success as a leader. These are profiles that have been largely unwritten, until now.

Priscilla Stephan has been an innate guide and leader in every role she's played, from her early days as a Program Officer at the World Wildlife Fund and then at the Inter-American Development Bank in Washington DC, where she worked with high-level government leaders for a decade, creating new environmental policies that would support a sustainable planet. Ultimately, Priscilla has now been called to her soul's work: coaching women entrepreneurs and leaders to live their purpose by growing world-changing businesses. When I heard Priscilla was bringing forward a leadership model based on foundational archetypes of the human soul, it was clear that she had fully stepped into her own right livelihood and new paradigm of leadership. The integration of her life's path is evidenced in this profound body of work she has ushered in and shares with us all now.

It's time for us to flip the script on leadership and call forth the wisdom that has been hidden in plain sight for centuries. This is a new paradigm that includes all facets of self and recognizes that while we all embody paradox in our own way we also have attributes that prioritize and shine, guiding others. Our journey through the leadership archetypes is not static. We are not born one style of leader and remain there through life's learning journeys unchanged. Instead we move through the archetypes as we cultivate ourselves in the direction of our life's purpose. We are not one-dimensional; we are like a full wheel of experiences, an amalgamation of expertise and insight, of intuition and intellect, of vision and imagination.

Exploring the leadership archetypes Priscilla identifies in this book and in her work lays a strong foundation for better understanding ourselves, each other, and our place in the world. Not only do we learn about who we are and how we can create more effective impact, but embracing our own leadership archetype helps us navigate the *journey* of leading, so that we can leave a legacy of other activated and aligned leaders in our wake.

The times ahead require that we shed old hierarchical models of leading that include dominance, shame, blame, and perpetuate the very trauma humanity is seeking to heal. Instead, we embrace a model that creates the space for deep healing and community repair and invites us to envision a world that is more unified, more mutually beneficial, and leaves no one behind. This is a future I believe we have the opportunity to craft with one another going forward, with the help of good information, good vision, and good tools. And Priscilla's work offers all three.

As you journey forward into this text, access the courage to release what you have been told. Summon deeper inquiry about the inner drumbeat that is calling you forward to your highest self. Let yourself be guided by the words and the ancient wisdom into a *remembering* of your true self. I believe there is a gift within each of us, and that those gifts can be cultivated and deepened through these pages.

Welcome to a new way. Thank you for the good work in the world you will leave in your wake.

Lindsay Pera
CEO & Founder of the Modern Mystics Institute

Praise

"Priscillas's approach is so timely with the needs of today, and her wisdom; timeless. I highly recommend reading this book BEFORE you write your business plan, build your founding team, or seek outside capital. So many gems. I think this book will change the game in how businesses are built."

– Kari Warberg Block, CEO & Founder, EarthKind®

"A soulful and enriching guide that challenges you to deeply connect with your personal leadership style, providing the often-missed bridge from inspiration to action".

– Miki Agrawal, Founder of WILD, THINX, and TUSHY and
#1 best-selling author of *Disrupt-her* and *Do Cool Sh*t*

"The Soulfluent® Leadership Business Guide is a great source to help you discover more of who you are. The Soulfluent® Strategist Archetype describes me to a T! I've learned how my archetype can be used to create ease and simplicity. I can be more hands-off while allowing others to support me with my day-to-day. This has helped to create more space so that I can be more creative in my life and business and truly trust my ideas and bring them to fruition."

– Nicole Richardson, Online Launch Strategist

"Priscilla is a gifted guide and super savvy force of light. You could not find a better provider to take your successful business to the next level into TOTAL alignment with your divine path and purpose."

– Lindsay Pera, Business Strategist & Founder, Modern Mystic Institute

"You don't have to hate marketing anymore. This book gives you radical permission to do business on your terms. Because, as this archetypal marketing system makes clear, working with your personality and preferences – instead of against them – is the only way that works. This book and framework is hot-shit amazing!"

– Kelly Diels, Culture Maker, Coach

Preface

As an Intuitive Business Strategist and Creator of the Soulfluent® Leadership Archetypes, I help mission-based entrepreneurs find their zones of genius, step into powerful leadership, and live their purpose profitably.

I work with leaders from a wide range of industries who have one thing in common: the desire to create a global impact and live a life of purpose without sacrificing their time, relationships, or well-being.

I have helped hundreds of soulful women entrepreneurs from newbies to owners of six-figure and seven-figure businesses thrive past their upper limit and become confident, empowered, and unstoppable leaders in their business—**and in the pages ahead, I hope to help you, too.**

Working collaboratively with my clients who are self-proclaimed visionaries and rebels, I combine a powerful duo of soul guidance from the Akashic Records with practical business strategy that gives them the ultimate edge to lead from a higher purpose with greater self-trust and without getting lost in the minutiae. This allows them to step into their next level of leadership and to create more impact and profits with grace and joy without working harder or burning out.

I believe that the path to growing a successful and sustainable, mission-driven business with meaning and purpose starts from within and by leading from your soul.

As your guide, **I help you navigate the mystery and confusion around your next steps in business and help you get clear on your soul's vision for leadership.**

After a decade of doing this work, here's what I know to be true: **Dreams and businesses don't create fulfillment and success. Alignment does.** This happens when your values, your dreams, your well-being, and the way you really want to run your business are congruent. This is holistic success—and it's how you live when you lead from your soul.

Like many of the clients I attract, I am an edge-worker, a term coined by Charles Eisenstein to describe vanguards who midwife ground-breaking paradigms that usher in a better world. Together, I help my clients navigate the exhilarating and at times choppy waters involved in birthing frameworks and entire businesses that transcend the mainstream and create a better world for all.

Combining the intuitive and logical worlds can accelerate growth, minimize futile guess-work, maximize profits, and support deep alignment with your soul's calling.

You are here to change the world. It's my mission to support you in doing that more powerfully and joyfully. Your soul provides the EDGE that you are looking for, and I can help you access it.

For these reasons, I am so happy that you have found your way to the *Soulfluent® Leadership Guide*. It's my hope that this work will help you not only grow your business in a meaningful and fulfilling way but also support you as you grow into your fullest expression as a leader and embody the language of your soul's leadership: your Soulfluent® Leadership Archetype.

In 2016, I started to channel in the Akashic Records[1] what would become the Soulfluent® Leadership Archetypes. Never in my wildest dreams did I think I'd one day be guiding people in becoming powerful, soul-driven leaders. To me, leadership was a stuffy topic laden with images of intimidating old men in suits telling people what to do. And I wanted nothing to do with that! On this journey, so much of my personal work (and that of my clients) has involved deprogramming old beliefs and preconceived notions of what it means to be a leader and giving myself permission to define what leadership means to me. And your journey will likely follow a similar path.

The Soulfluent® Leadership framework defines leadership as contribution. This means that we are all leaders because we all naturally contribute to the world. Whether you are a janitor or schoolteacher, a pilot, scientist, mother, or entrepreneur, you have within your soul's blueprint a unique set of talents, gifts, and abilities to make the world a better place.

---

1   Your Akashic Records, also called your soul's records or "Book of Life," are the complete documentation of everything you've experienced in every lifetime since your soul's creation. Every dream, joy, pattern, relationship, struggle, desire, and success is found within its sacred pages. The Akashic Records are a sacred space of Healing, Truth, and Love, intended to help you align with your soul's purpose, release blocks and patterns of self-sabotage, and create a life of bliss that aligns with who you truly, undeniably are.

This body of work supports leaders to stay grounded in their vision and primed to lead themselves and their organization with boldness, courage, and sustainable growth while creating a world that works for everyone.

Perhaps what I love the most about this work is that it's not here to tell you what to do. Rather, it's designed to help you understand yourself better and thereby consciously choose how you wish to show up and contribute in a way that's innately your own.

Too often, we refrain from stepping into a leadership role, for fear that we will do harm and turn into leaders we would never want to emulate, simply because we haven't been shown how to lead in a healthy way.

The good news is that you already know how to lead. This is because you have within you a soul blueprint for your unique brand of contribution. You just haven't been introduced to it or shown how to weave it into your life in a way that feels safe and natural—a way that aligns with your values.

This is the beauty of the Soulfluent® Leadership Archetypes. By helping you to know yourself more intimately—your strengths, your pitfalls, and what your unique contribution can create (without burning you out or compromising what matters most to you)—you can feel more confident saying yes to your leadership while staying true to yourself.

For me, discovering that I am a Soulfluent® Mystic Archetype deepened my understanding of my healing power to hold space for others. This gave me the life-changing permission to stop trying too hard, to allow my energy to be a catalyst for magic, and, more importantly, to trust myself (despite my crippling Mystic self-doubt) to birth this body of work into the world.

Past clients of my Leadership Roundtables who have aligned their businesses with their primary Soulfluent® Archetype have seen exponential growth in their confidence, visibility, and potency as business owners, leaders, and changemakers. When you align and lead from your Soulfluent® Leadership Archetype, absolutely anything is possible, even in a short period of time: restructuring business models and adding in new revenue streams that sell out in a few weeks...tweaking existing offers into virtual experiences that reach a global audience...launching community experiences that highlight business best practices, inclusion, and charity work in one space...closing a life-altering, highly lucrative real estate deal. And these are just a few examples of the limitless possibilities.

I'm especially proud that the natural byproduct of my years of helping clients lead from their soul in life and business is the freedom to enjoy *all* areas of their life while earning a great living and making the world a better place.

I truly believe in the magnificence of the human spirit and in the power of infinite possibilities when we stay open, say yes, and let our souls lead the way.

When we know ourselves better, we lead better. And this is the contribution offered by the Soulfluent® Leadership framework.

It is my hope that this book will be a warm and steady companion by your bedside or desk, guiding you to the next level of business growth while keeping you in alignment with and true to your essence: your soul.

Whether you are a Soulfluent® Mystic, Visionary, Strategist, Explorer, or Divine Feminine Archetype, I'm excited to see how this guide will propel you on your path of soul leadership.

Welcome to Soulfluent® Leadership!

Now let's get started!

-Priscilla

Table of Contents

Introduction 1

The Leadership Ascension Journey 5

The Soulfluent® Leadership Archetypes 11

How to Get the Most from This Guide 13

Overview Matrix of the Soulfluent® Leadership Archetypes 21

Descriptors for Each Soulfluent® Leadership Archetype 25

Matrix: Archetype Kryptonite + Antidote 27

The Soulfluent® Mystic Leadership Archetype 29

- Overview of the Soufluent® Mystic Leader
- Vision
- Manifestation Style
- Branding
- Marketing
- Business Model
- Team Building
- Mindset
- Mystic at a Glance
- Reflection Questions

The Soulfluent® Visionary Leadership Archetype 59

- Overview of the Soulfluent® Visionary Leader
- Vision
- Manifestation Style
- Branding
- Marketing
- Business Model
- Team Building
- Mindset
- Visionary at a Glance
- Reflection Questions

The Soulfluent® Strategist Leadership Archetype................................ 89
- Overview of the Soulfluent® Strategist
- Vision
- Manifestation Style
- Branding
- Marketing
- Business Model
- Team Building
- Mindset
- Strategist at a Glance
- Reflection Questions

The Soulfluent® Explorer Leadership Archetype................................ 117
- Overview of the Soulfluent® Explorer
- Vision
- Manifestation Style
- Branding
- Marketing
- Business Model
- Team Building
- Mindset
- Explorer at a Glance
- Reflection Questions

The Soulfluent® Divine Feminine Leadership Archetype................. 149
- Overview of the Soulfluent® Divine Feminine
- Vision
- Manifestation Style
- Branding
- Marketing
- Business Model
- Team Building
- Mindset
- Divine Feminine at a Glance
- Reflection Questions

Conclusion... 181
Take the Quiz... 185
About the Author... 197
Acknowledgments... 199

Introduction
Why now is the time to rise up and to lead with soul

More than ever before, there is a collective call to create a new normal. Now is the time to remove old structures of traditional leadership that were hierarchical, exclusive, and ego-driven, replacing them with new paradigms that are sustainable, holistic, inclusive, compassionate, and that reflect choices where everyone, including the planet, wins.

Change is afoot, and we know that we are the catalysts for change. But change requires, first, a new level of leadership within ourselves, followed by a new level of leadership externally.

We have deep questions that are inviting us to lead ourselves first, then to lead others.

This is the beauty of Soulfluent® Leadership. It helps you to understand the language of your soul's leadership, including personal biases and egoic urges, and how to access this wisdom consciously in all that you do. By leading from their innate strengths, leaders lead more freely, bringing healing and positive change to their communities, organizations, and companies that supports a humane world where everyone thrives.

Our unique soul path for leadership and impact awaits us and the time is now to define what leadership ultimately means to each of us.

What is Soulfluent® Leadership?

It's identifying, accessing, and speaking the leadership language of your soul. Doing so allows you to be the fullest and most natural expression of yourself in your work and to lead organizations, businesses, groups, and yourself from an energy of high integrity and truth that magnetizes people and opportunities to you.

Soulfluent® leaders are highly aware of the current realities of the world while actively bridge-walking themselves and others into new horizons of what's possible.

In their efforts to help create a better world for everyone, they actively make choices through the lens of "we" versus just "me." And this is the beauty of Soulfluent® Leadership. It's a call to lead that both elevates and supports us all through the practice of listening to and following our soul's guidance.

What's possible when you step into your Soulfluent® Leadership?

- Make bold moves that shift the trajectory of your business without working harder.
- Maximize your profits while creating a culture that works for everyone.
- Grow your community and lead your movement to create the change you know is possible.
- Create a legacy that fulfills your soul's work and changes lives.

You do all of this while fully living your deepest, most fulfilling life without sacrificing your time, relationships, or health.

Traditional Leadership vs. Soulfluent® Leadership

Traditional leadership often tells people what to do based on antiquated models of external markers of success that can result in working harder, doing more, and following the rules.

This sometimes leads to burnout, a lack of fulfillment, and endlessly striving to get ahead at the expense of your joy and what matters most to you. It's "me" focused and generates competition where someone always loses.

Soulfluent® Leadership is soul-driven contribution that supports the greater good. More specifically, it's using your soul's guidance and purpose to consciously create a meaningful and sustainable world where everyone thrives. This is what I call a 360° win.

TRADITIONAL LEADERSHIP (ego-driven)	SOULFLUENT® LEADERSHIP (soul-driven: a 360° win)
hustle	nourishing flow
burned out	inspired
working harder	working smarter
overwhelmed	fulfilled
fitting in	joyfully expressed
trapped	expansive
reactive	proactive
unsustainable	sustainable
hierarchical	inclusive
competitive (me)	collaborative (we)

Copyright 2022. Soulfluent LLC

Soulfluent® Leadership is an invitation to consciously contribute to a more humane world by taking full responsibility for your path, your choices, and how you choose to share your talents.

The Leadership Ascension Journey

What is the process that will allow you to step into the next level of leadership and business?

During my own leadership ascension process I discovered that it takes **an identity shift.** In essence, a new version of oneself.

I wish I'd known this when I found myself stuck in an 18-month metamorphosis that left me questioning everything I held dear. At the time, I felt stagnant, like a total failure (cue the dark nights of the soul).

Looking back, I wish I'd had **context** for that period so I'd have known how to reap its gifts in a way that was less painful, that made me feel less alone. I believe that knowing what to expect on the journey can empower you to stay the course, confident that even when you're feeling lost and scared, you're not off course. Quite the opposite: those challenging moments let you know you're exactly where you need to be.

I've asked my guides to share with me this Ascension Model, which illustrates the path that so many of us—as leaders, as those who answer the call to leadership—go through. Every leadership journey is unique. This model describes my ascension experience and that of my clients, so you will be best served by taking what resonates with you, and leaving anything that does not.

You'll notice that this Ascension Model is called NEW Level, not next level—because you will emerge from the process a new version of yourself—clearer about your vision and your values, aligned with how you want to show up in the world.

Now let's dive a little deeper into each phase, along with the gifts and challenges they bring.

Welcome to the Soulfluent® New Level Leader Ascension Model

This model is designed to help you understand exactly where you are on your evolutionary leadership journey so that you can keep your sanity, deepen your grace and compassion, and increase your potency as you grow into the next level of contribution and leadership.

The six phases of this model help you identify and contextualize where you are along the path, allowing you to **maximize the potential of each stage.**

Soulfluent® New Level Leader Ascension Model

6. New Level Leader	I have a new perspective
5. Restructuring	It's in process
4. Identity Crisis	Old patterns dissolve
3. Consciously Say Yes	Can I really handle this?
2. Denial	This isn't for me
1. Awakening Initiation	You feel the call

Copyright 2022. Soulfluent LLC

Stage 1: The Awakening/ Initiation: You feel the call

Perhaps you find yourself feeling a pull or a nudge, or maybe a major life event causes you to break free from your old ways of doing things, of seeing life or yourself. You feel a call to lead, to contribute, to do things differently.

Stage 2: Denial: This isn't for me

This is where you may be unsure about answering the call or whether you're cut out for what's ahead. You keep telling yourself things like: "I don't know if I'm equipped for this. What should I do? And do I really even want to do this?" Contemplating the pros and cons can serve you well before you decide how to answer the call to lead.

Stage 3: Conscious Decision to Say "Yes": Can I really handle this?

After careful contemplation, and in spite of the uncertain road ahead, this is where you consciously choose to say yes to the call to lead. The nature of that call can be as varied as a desire to start a non-profit, to share a bolder new message in your business, to travel, to leave a job, to pursue a promotion, to show up differently in a personal or professional relationship. At this stage, you decide to jump in with both feet even though you don't yet know the "hows" of the path ahead.

Stage 4: Identity Crisis: Old patterns dissolve

Like the chrysalis stage in a butterfly's growth, this is the most transformative and challenging stage. It's a **liminal space** where you are no longer who you were but not yet entirely the new self you are becoming. You may find yourself very inward-focused, slightly confused, not quite able to understand the deep shifts happening under the surface … and yet by the end of the process you will emerge a gorgeous butterfly poised to soar and share your magic with the world.

This stage is deeply transformative because your old patterns dissolve and new ways of being take shape as you set aside and move beyond old beliefs, patterns, and limitations.

More poignantly, this stage is where your deepest fears of unworthiness, self-doubt, scarcity, of being an imposter rise to the surface to be examined and transmuted.

You may find yourself wondering: Who am I to lead? What will it take for me to step up to the plate—and am I ready for it? What if I disappoint myself or others? What if people judge me or ridicule me? Can I even make a difference? What am I actually good at? Am I willing to truly commit to the path? What if I fail? Or succeed?

These are some of the deep, dark-night-of-the-soul questions that emerge. Maintaining a healthy state of mind during this phase, which may last up to a year, depends on your ability to **embrace curiosity and explore all the questions emerging with grace, self-compassion, and awe.**

During this stage, patterns that stem from more ego-driven tendencies and from childhood may come up. For me, I had to honestly consider whether my motivations to lead related more to my need to prove myself and my worth (my ego) or to the idea of helping others for the sake of the cause itself.

Questions that I asked myself included:

- "What is my leadership asking of me?"
- "Who do I need to be in order to be a steward of my work and vision?"
- "What does being a leader mean to me?"
- "What kind of a leader am I?"
- "What role do I play in sharing my work so I can do it authentically—without feeling like an imposter?"

The more openly you lean into the questions, the more richness you will harvest from this fertile time of growth. **A sense of peace can arise when you trust that your emergence process is a natural and healthy one that will result in tremendous growth, even when it feels super uncomfortable.**

An important insight I gained throughout this process was realizing that, in my work, my role is as a **guide for others** to contemplate and to embrace their own brand of leadership—**not as the "expert" with all the answers.** Moreover, I accepted that my approach and life experiences are more than rich enough to warrant sharing my work right now—without needing more "impressive" accolades, titles, or accomplishments to somehow make me ready or worthy. These distinctions freed me to be myself with true integrity, confident in my ability to share my body of work without feeling like a fraud or an imposter.

Stage 5: Restructuring: The emergence of insight and answers from within

In this phase you will start to notice shifts in your thinking and behaviors, and you will begin to feel lighter, less stuck. Finally, you can see the first hints of light at the end of the tunnel. You feel more encouraged and hopeful about who you are becoming and the path forward.

Stage 6: New Level Leader

You have emerged with a new perspective, conscious of a palpable shift in identity deep within and anchored into your being. You find yourself embodying new energies and insights, feeling more confident in who you are and the direction your life is heading. You are confident in your ability to move forward and prosper, making the difference that only you can.

The Soulfluent® Leadership Archetypes

Mystic | Visionary | Strategist | Explorer | Divine Feminine

Understanding your Soulfluent® Leadership Archetype

An Archetype includes the energies, patterns, beliefs, and programming that are present in the collective unconscious. While we each carry within us the potency of multiple Archetypes at any given time, there is generally a dominant Soulfluent® Leadership Archetype present in our leadership style. When you understand this primary energy, you access keen insights into your personal strengths and shadows so you can create and lead more effectively.

Archetypes also illuminate your innate brilliance and reveal how to apply it in every area of your life and business to create more of what you desire with greater ease. I call these Archetypes your Soul DNA.

The more you trust that your Soul DNA exists to be your ally (i.e., the more "soulfluent" you are), the easier your existence will be. Likewise, the more you collaborate with your own Soul Design and trust the good it can create, the prosperity it can afford, and the positive change it can evoke in the world, the easier life will be.

Look at your Soulfluent® Leadership Archetype as a way to guide you and expand your deepest desires rather than a way of limiting or defining you.

One of the incredible benefits of leading with your superpowers is that it enables you to understand on a deep level that **yes you CAN** make amazing money helping people using talents that come as naturally to you as breathing—and then you find that you're able to do exactly that. How could it get any better?

How to Get the Most from This Guide

For those who have worked with me through my Soulfluent® Leadership Roundtable, eight week intensive, or Private Mentoring Program, we've already identified your Soulfluent® Primary Archetype, your Secondary Archetype, and possibly even a third one. If so, feel free to turn directly to the appropriate section of this guide. If you haven't already identified your Primary Archetype and the concept is new to you, start by taking the quiz on page 185 of this book. Alternatively, you can take the quiz online at: **http://www.priscillastephan. com/quiz**.

You can also begin by exploring the section of the guide you feel most drawn to or read each section in order from beginning to end. Whichever way you choose, you'll gain immense value when you begin to integrate this information into your business. Starting on page 29 you'll find an overview of the basic principles for each Archetype, followed by a one-page summary of each Archetype at the end of each section.

Each Soulfluent® Leadership Archetype leads, informs, guides, and transmutes the leader. Likewise, your Archetype influences your vision, messaging, marketing, way of being, and manner of interacting with yourself and your clients, customers, team members, businesses, brand, industry, and the world.

My strong recommendation is to read beyond just your primary Archetype. While you will want to become fluent in it over time, there is wisdom and potency in also becoming familiar with the other Archetypes, as they reflect the leadership language of those nearest to you such as your assistant, your Chief Financial Officer, your Marketing Director, your Operations Strategist, to name a few. Becoming fluent, even if partially in *their* soul's leadership language, will create more fluidity, flow, and connection, which in turn creates a smoother business operation and overall efficiency.

As humans, we are always evolving and growing. Consequently, you may find that, over time, your Primary and Secondary Soulfluent® Leadership Archetypes may shift to some degree. Becoming familiar with all the Archetypes now can make it easier to tap into these slight shifts along your journey.

The power to alchemize your strengths into gold

To alchemize (definition): to transform the nature or properties of (something) by a seemingly magical process (Merriam-Webster dictionary).

This comprehensive guide provides direction on how to grow six aspects of your business: branding, marketing, manifesting, business model, team building, and leadership and money mindset.

You'll be able to more clearly see what you are creating through the strengths and challenges of your primary Archetype.

The insights about your Archetype allow you to alchemize your innate strengths and leadership style into gold both for your personal business as well as for the greater good. Think of these as your "Alchemy Codes."

It's important to remember that every human contains all of the energies, and if you're like most people, you'll likely resonate with certain aspects of each Archetype. But don't let yourself get swept away in *all* of the energies.

> **Focus on your primary Soulfluent® Leadership Archetype and let that lead you on your path.**

Your Primary Soulfluent® Leadership Archetype will take you where you need to go faster, better, more soulfully, more efficiently, more powerfully, and with more compassion than trying to find your way through logic alone.

You're about to see how your Soulfluent® Leadership Archetype will light the way for your business through tangible strategies, concrete words, particular colors, and energetic nuances that will become a beacon enabling your ideal audience to find you. All the while, your Archetype will help you grow, evolve, and transform into a radiant leader who's ready to soar.

How to use your Primary and Secondary Soulfluent® Leadership Archetypes

Your Primary Soulfluent® Leadership Archetype is the dominant energy guiding your most important decisions.

Your Secondary Archetype offers another helpful suite of energies, gifts, and guidance to complement those of your Primary Archetype. Think of them as stacking on each other and providing added nuance, potency, and guidance for your leadership.

Let's imagine that you are a dominant Soulfluent® Mystic Leadership Archetype and your Secondary Archetype is the Soulfluent® Visionary. In such a case, the Soulfluent® Visionary Archetype exists to remind you to focus on running your business with extraordinary efficiency and to heighten the boldness of your Soulfluent® Mystic message with fearlessness and focus.

Your Soulfluent® Visionary Archetype may also be an invitation to explore how you can streamline your offers and create simple systems in your business that allow for more leverage and automation so your operations can be more "hands off" without losing the all-important high-touch service. It's like a *Yes and*: *Yes* I can lead with my Mystic gifts *and* run my business even more efficiently and with a bolder message.

How this guide came about

One day a colleague who knew my work said to me: "Wouldn't it be great to have a guide your clients could give to their branding person, business coach, team members, graphic designer, or copy and social media manager and say, 'Here! Just use this to create this part of my business in alignment with my Soulfluent® Leadership Archetype?'"

Think about how much time and money you'll save. Think about how much more effective you will be.

My colleague's imaginative inquiry was all it took. I began to channel the material in the Akashic Records immediately, and you're looking at the results.

How your Soulfluent® Leadership Archetype influences three key business levers—your business model, your message, and your money flows

As you read through the business guide, keep in mind that your Soulfluent® Leadership Archetype is a catalyst to alchemize three core levers in your work that will, in turn, transform how you show up, lead, grow, and ultimately monetize your mission from a space of deep inner alignment.

Your Business Model: The Driver

Your business model is the driver, aka the engine, of your work. It's the structure through which you service your clients, through which you receive and service payments, and how you show up most powerfully in your work. It informs: a) your role in the company; b) the team members that you hire and their roles; c) your core products, programs, and offers; and d) ultimately how you leverage your time and resources to provide a high-value, high-touch experience to your customers without burning out or compromising your valuable time.

Your Message: The Heart

Your message transcends what you become known for. It's how you communicate with your customers through your energy, your body language, your style and tone of speaking, your relatability and resonance with your customer base, and your ability to deeply connect with yourself as you simultaneously connect with your audience.

Your message is the heart of your work and impacts how it is received, perceived, and integrated into the hearts of those receptive to it.

Your Money: The Reward

This is the outcome of your hard work. Most would say that this is the desired reward for the alignment you achieve by building and growing your business in alignment with your Soulfluent® Leadership Archetype. Money flows are expanded and remain consistent when the other elements of your business are aligned with your Soulfluent® Leadership Archetype. The money you create allows you to then reinvest in your business, support causes that are meaningful, and enjoy an abundant lifestyle. These are just a few of the benefits of doing your soul's work in a way that is so authentically expressed and meaningful to you and to the planet.

Alchemizing the inner and outer game: The ultimate edge

Mastering the Inner Game

The beauty of working with Archetypes is that they provide a framework to help you deeply understand yourself as you transmute and work in flow with your inner game. This smooths the way for you to take bigger risks and show up more powerfully in your elevated leadership.

Integrating your Archetype into your work gives you the tools to move past fears and self-doubt, to speak up courageously, to be fully seen, to withstand judgment, to hold firmly and gracefully to boundaries, and to maintain integrity and groundedness in the face of challenges. When you understand potential pitfalls, you can proactively rely upon a toolbox of aligned strategies that will keep you leading in all your potency. In this way, hitting a snag is just a momentary hold-up; rather than getting stuck, you circumvent the obstacle and move forward into elevated levels of soul-driven leadership, doing your part to create a world where everyone thrives.

Taking Action + Changing the World

Alignment is the ultimate tool for maximizing your resources. This is because the natural side effects of alignment include efficiency and optimization. In a world where time, money, and energy seem to be at a premium, taking action in alignment with your Soulfluent® Leadership Archetype inherently means that you are only spending and prioritizing your valuable resources on what will create the greatest outcomes for your Archetype, rather than wasting time on strategies, business models, team members, and customer products and experiences that don't work for your company and your big-vision goals.

Growing your business in alignment with your Soulfluent® Leadership Archetype is a one hundred percent soul-customized and optimized approach to saving time, money, and energy so you get the most out of your efforts and spend the bulk of your time in your zone of genius, making the world a better place for everyone.

What my clients are saying......

"What I realized was that I was operating from the Visionary Archetype which was actually burning me out because I was overlooking the energy that was calling me into something new: The Divine Feminine. With Priscilla's help, I gave myself permission to lean into my natural talent of collaboration and creating community and to get paid really well for it.

Knowing my Soulfluent® Leadership Archetype clarified my next steps, and for the first time, I see a viable, lucrative business model as a possibility that's generative, fulfilling, and an incredible contribution to humanity as well."

~Angella Johnson
Creator of of the Intuitive Marketing Matrix™

Important Notes:

The guidance in this book is merely a suggestion. Do not feel obligated to apply every piece of advice to your business; after all, every business has its own unique essence, message, and tone.

As you have likely noticed, this guide is jam-packed with information, and at first you might find yourself a bit overwhelmed about how to integrate it into your business.

Focus on your Primary Soulfluent® Leadership Archetype first and take the guide section by section. And, most importantly, remember to have fun!

A few extra Archetype resources for you:

- For a **10-minute overview video** of all of the five Soulfluent® Leadership Archetypes (think of it as a quick refresher) visit: **https://priscillastephan.com/quiz-overview**.

- To listen to the **Doing Business Thru Your Soulfluent® Leadership Archetype Interview Series** where five entrepreneurs share insights on how they are leading through their specific Archetype in business, visit: **www.priscillastephan.com/interviews**.

- Spend some time reviewing **The Soulfluent® Leadership Archetype Overview Matrix (on page 21).** This delivers all the key content you need at your fingertips to alchemize your Primary Archetype's strengths into gold.

Now, let's dive into the pages of this guide and get you on your way to expanding your business with greater ease.

P.S.: If you are already a private client, this is what we'll cover in our work together. If you're not yet a private client and would like to explore how I can support you, schedule your clarity call here: **www.priscillastephan.com/letstalk**.

Overview Matrix of the Soulfluent® Leadership Archetypes

	Mystic	Visionary	Strategist	Explorer	Divine Feminine
Motivation	Elevate consciousness, facilitate harmony & healing.	Disrupt status quo, innovate.	Create new systems & processes that support the greater good.	Envision, explore, & expand new possibilities; activate imagination.	Build community, love, collaboration, equality. Bring forth flow & harmony.
Vision of the World	People operate from higher consciousness in zones of genius.	Super-efficient with systems that support the greater good.	Egalitarian with efficient & inclusive systems.	Freedom to be safe, creative, adventurous, & curious.	Global community—working together for the betterment of all with love, joy, & nourishment.
Manifestation Style	Desire. Believe. Actualize. Let go of the notion of time. Trust the process.	Believe. Call into form. Make it happen now.	Slow. Steady. Calm. Solitary. Deliberate & researched.	Fast & experiential. Keep trying & refining. A catalyst.	Quick creations & collaborations. Bold, intentional, fun.
Branding	Healing, harmony, purpose, peace.	Bold, outspoken, disruptive, unapologetic.	Data- & process-oriented explanations, real-life examples.	Experiential, imaginative, curious. Connect with possibility.	Flow, nature, connection, community, collaboration, love. Inspiring new vision.
Marketing	Gives context for journey to audience at different levels. Simple framework. Transformation. Healing.	Disrupts. Loud. Attention-grabbing. Makes bold promises. Takes a clear stand.	Invites big-picture thinking & efficiency. Precise, thorough.	Invites into adventures; experiential. Asks questions.	Invites into a better experience that also serves the greater good. Teaches & guides.

	Mystic	**Visionary**	**Strategist**	**Explorer**	**Divine Feminine**
Business Model	Diverse. Teach, heal, facilitate. Showcase your brilliance & give client options.	Spacious, leveraged (good systems & automation). A "well-oiled machine."	Shares your (mostly behind-the-scenes) brilliance. Teacher, guide.	Spacious + leveraged (serving larger groups without extra time expenditure) with diverse offerings. Supports your adventurous lifestyle.	Leveraged, community-driven opportunities, joint ventures. Spacious, diverse.
Offer Types	Diverse: 1:1, 1:many, groups, courses, retreats. Inner work & personal development.	1:many, targeted to client level & leveraged *or* some high-touch outcome-driven. Flagship offers = main income at key times of year. Outcome-driven.	Prefer 1:many vs. 1:1 in order to focus on big picture. High-level mentorship; membership, trainings.	Retreats, camps, travel. Tight containers with accelerated results. Experiential, nature-centric offers that evoke the imagination; can be sustainable through series-based offers.	Highly leveraged group programs. High-touch, outcome-focused, potent results that showcase your teaching. Community-based & driven by the greater good.
Team	Your team gives you time alone to make decisions & connect to intuitive guidance. Gives you informed, low-pressure input.	You're a fast decision-maker & don't want to spend time explaining the vision to team.	You're built to work in teams, but work better alone. Team allows you to focus on your ideas.	You need freedom, adventure, & people around you. Small team helps you create & connect without getting lost in or overthinking details. With larger teams, tend to interact mostly with key members.	Take time to build trust & communication with your team. Your dream team is loyal, creative, & collaborative.

	Mystic	Visionary	Strategist	Explorer	Divine Feminine
Mindset	Stay focused on positive outcome to avoid self-doubt. Boundaries—clear work hours & time off—keep your energy high & inspiration flowing.	You can feel alone. Have people around who believe in your vision, encourage you, & help you keep up momentum.	You carry the weight of the world on your shoulders. Time away from work, in nature, with friends is crucial.	Your mind & imagination need stimulation. Do what makes you feel alive, free, & engaged in possibility—avoid naysayers.	Spacious self-care helps you regain perspective, be inspired, & have your best ideas. Take time to celebrate your creations & to retreat & relax solo or with friends.
Systems/ Automation	Simple, clear, defined at all levels of customer service, tech, team. Onboarding, contracts, email sequences, opt-ins, payment.	Clear start-to-finish pipeline of offers. Org chart of team & roles. Offers are mostly hands-off; marketing & delivery are automated.	Hands-off in day-to-day ops. Focus on big picture & tech pieces. Team does backend & customer interface.	Delegate so you can focus on creating, imagining, & connecting. Team handles implementation, backend, & tech details.	Simple structures that allow (creative) flow are critical—online scheduling, working hours, team to handle client matters so you stay in flow & out of the details.
Content Creation	Simple, heartfelt, highly repurposed. Visually compelling, colorful, with symbols. Insight & story-driven (personal stories, client testimonials). Written (blogs) & spoken (podcasts, events, trainings, guest speakers). Pick one core path per outlet, stick with it, hone your voice.	Efficiency is key. Batch content creation. Schedule & repurpose in all media channels. Bold quotes, brand colors, thought-provoking. Content & images disrupt. "Edgy"; pushes buttons.	Masterfully distill complex ideas into tangible concepts. Process- & data-oriented. You create, team manages. Eye-catching, inviting. Shows uniqueness & directly supports audience.	Share your insights, relatable stories, & wild adventures from your heart in writing or audio. Let go of perfectionism. Be consistent in 1–3 core outlets. Use photos & quotes to conjure adventure, imagination. Feels like a travel journal.	Content is appealing, provocative, highly teachable, & thought-provoking. A natural storyteller, you write a lot of content, but co-creation is good for you, so delegate strategic thinking to team. Diversity in outlets/platforms. Branded, consistent, engaging, & interactive.

	Mystic	Visionary	Strategist	Explorer	Divine Feminine
Superpowers (SP)/ Kryptonite (K)/ Antidote (A)	SP: Intuitive, healing, creative abilities K: Self-doubt A: Be authentic	SP: Disruptor, out-of-the-box strategist K: Isolation, fitting in A: Be vulnerable	SP: Precise, persistent, innovative K: Overthinking + self-doubt A: Trust yourself + have fun	SP: Dreamer, connector, catalyst K: Many interests, naysayers, impatience A: Take action, form inner circle, trust self	SP: Community-builder, connector, catalyst K: Over-giving A: Practice more self-care
Keys to Success	Remember your 3 Ds: Diversity Delegation Downtime	Be efficient in making offers & in overall delivery. Be highly leveraged & automated. Deliver a bold, clear message.	Let team implement ideas. Focus on bigger picture. Lightness/ fun keep the machine operating. Trust your creative (out-of-the-box) solutions to status-quo problems.	Your creative process takes you from idea to launch. Delegate implementation to your team. Stay focused & away from details.	Focus on your "why." Be willing to do things differently & more creatively. Collaborate, co-create, & receive. Implement leveraged business model, offers, & operations.

Descriptors for Each Soulfluent® Leadership Archetype

This summary, which highlights the top qualities and roles of each Soulfluent® Leadership Archetype, will help you distinguish their unique characteristics.

Mystic
Intuitive
Messenger
Oracle
Healer
Teacher
Guide

Visionary
Disruptor
Out-of-the-box thinker
Efficiency-driven
Outspoken
Innovative
Bold
Trailblazer

Strategist
Precise
Detail-oriented
Process-, systems-
and data-driven
Sees big picture and
day-to-day tasks
Teacher
Creative
Innovative
Persistent
Patient
Caring

Explorer
Connector
Visionary
Dreamer
Driven by possibilities
Guide
Catalyst
Adventurer (lives and
leads experientially)

Divine Feminine
Collaborator
Connector
Co-creator
Inclusive
Community builder
Mastery
Flow
Receiver

Matrix: Archetype Kryptonite + Antidote

Superpowers + strategy for overcoming difficulties for each Soulfluent® Leadership Archetype

Each Soulfluent® Leadership Archetype has its own unique strengths and challenges. Here are the most common ones, along with suggestions for navigating challenges to ensure you can operate at your best.

Kryptonite (definition): An existing belief, habit, or pattern that can significantly derail you when you are creating or stepping into something new or challenging.

Antidote (definition): A new way of being that allows you to be more self-expressed and confident moving forward.

ARCHETYPE	SUPERPOWERS (your innate gifts)	KRYPTONITE (what stands in the way of leading)	ANTIDOTE (the path to taking action and being fully self-expressed)
Mystic	Intuitive, creative, healing	Self-doubt, fear of embracing spiritual gifts	Be authentic
Visionary	Disruptor, efficient, outspoken	Fitting in, isolation	Be vulnerable
Strategist	Creative solutions, precise, connects dots	Overthinking, self-doubt	Trust in self and the process Enjoy lighthearted fun
Explorer	Dreamer, catalyst, adventurer	Too many interests at once Naysayers Impatience	Take action Form an inner circle Stay grounded Trust the unfolding process
Divine Feminine	Community builder, connector, catalyst	Over-giving	Practice more self-care

EMPOWERING QUESTIONS TO STAY ENERGIZED BY YOUR ARCHETYPE

As you learn to lean into and lead from your Soulfluent® Leadership Archetype, one of the most powerful tools you can use is your Archetype's antidote.

The clarifying questions below can help you feel more comfortable with the energy of your Archetype's antidote and the many ways it can empower you:

Soulfluent® Mystic:
How can I feel safe befriending and sharing my spiritual gifts?

Soulfluent® Visionary:
How can I embrace the boldness of my message and
still ensure my human need to fit in and to belong is met?

Soulfluent® Strategist:
How can I trust my creative solutions to problems and
not be deterred by pushback and criticism from my peers?

Soulfluent® Explorer:
How can I embrace the benefits of having multiple interests
in a world that wants to put me into a box?

Soulfluent® Divine Feminine:
How can I find balance between staying present and in flow
and welcoming the freedom that structure provides?

The
Soulfluent®
Mystic
Leadership
Archetype

*"I lead by using my intuition
to create transformation."*

Overview of the Soulfluent®
Mystic Leader

As a Mystic Leader, you are here to transform the status quo by elevating consciousness, inviting people into new possibilities by way of your intuitive, healing, and creative gifts. You will be misunderstood, you may be criticized and called crazy, and you definitely won't fit into the status quo. This is by design. Trust your Archetype—collaborate with it and remember the good it is creating.

Dominant Motivation to Lead:
To create transformation; to elevate consciousness by facilitating well-being and harmony.

Gifts:
Intuitive, healing, creative, healer, teacher, activist, truth-teller, shape-shifter, alchemist, change-maker.

Challenges:
Hard on self, low self-esteem, self-doubt, money challenges, overburdened with worries of others, tries to save others.

The Soulfluent® Mystic's Vision

The Mystic's vision for both the world and their leadership is well-being, joy, peace, and elevated consciousness.

Mystics elevate consciousness by evoking harmony and well-being.

Soulfluent® Mystic Manifestation Style

Mystics are courageous and always envisioning what's next. You call on the support of guides, angels, and invisible beings for ongoing support. Mystics are natural manifestors. When you trust yourself to manifest your pure desire, and you clear the way for it to show up even better than you imagined, you are golden.

The more quickly you are able to embrace your manifestation style, instead of fearing its potency or not clearly asking for what you really want, the more you will enjoy the actualization of your desires.

Everything has its own process. You will savor the process of manifestation much more when you keep a clean energy around your desire, maintain an attitude of gratitude, and stay curious, asking questions that keep you in alignment with your desire.

Finally, Mystics manifest incredibly quickly, which means that it's important to be as ready as you can for what you desire *and* to view your own powers of creation from a place of gratitude and awe, rather than fear and angst. This will open up an attitude of *allowing*. While you are incredibly potent, dear Mystic, know that you are never given more power than you can handle.

Part of your edge in growing into manifestation will lie in your ability to trust what you are desiring and to stay in the energy of knowing it's already being taken care of. No matter how deep or how long you've had the desire, trusting that the Universe will open the doors in its own perfect timing, versus your own, will serve you well.

Mystic Manifestation Process:

- Clarify your pure desire.

- Call in support from invisible forces.

- Ask for your desire in its entirety. Don't piecemeal it based on what you think you can have.

- Visualize it and *feel* it throughout your body.

- Hold the energy of your desire and expand it out, then ask that energy to regenerate as needed in order to stay active.

- Bless the ask. Bless yourself. Bless the Universe. And bless the receiving of your desire, whenever and however it arrives, for it is already complete and on its way to you.

- Have fun creating. Surprise yourself with how wonderful your creations will be.

From here, detach and trust the process and yourself.

Release any expectation about the timing for the desire to come into form. Don't allow the illusion of time (i.e., your perception of tardiness) to cloud your ability to hold the inner knowing that everything is already taken care of.

Remember that there are infinite possibilities for how your desire may show up—and it will *always* be better than you imagine, so long as you don't try to intervene. Think of it as a cake in the oven; don't try to interfere with the alchemical magic by taking the cake out before it's fully baked.

Soulfluent® Mystic Branding

Brand Message

Transformation: There is a better way to live life on purpose. Speak to the deepest, most desired outcome.

Brand Words

As you browse through the following branding words, keep in mind that it would be impossible to use all of them in your messaging and copywriting. Circle the words that you feel the most resonance with, and use these as your gauge for everything you create in your business.

Brand Words

alchemy, alchemist	transformation	healing	purpose (-driven)	love	kindness	compassion	a new and better ways to do things	soul (-led)	disruptor
disruption	visionary	harmony	magic	self-love	self-worth	medicine	self-trust	inner work	inner depths
ritual	a new way/new world	a new paradigm	new systems	sacred	you know the way	path	illuminate	carve	guide
inform	interject	collaborate	nudge	show	change-maker	way-maker	vision	possibility	opportunity
believe	trust	now	inspiration	Divine	Divinity	spirituality	spirit	heart	from the heart
heart-centered/driven	feeling/sensing/perceiving	alignment	energy	soul-aligned	Divine Timing	Divine Truth	Divine Energy	wholeness	whole
well-being	wellness	health	peace	regression	community	oneness	oracle	Mystic	teacher
activist	trouble-rouser	travel	traveler	gypsy	feminine	leadership	Leader	conscious	consciousness
awareness	aware	enlightened	enlightenment	energy	trailblazer	old soul	religions	timeless	effortless
ease	tuned in	tapped in	unicorn	intuition	intuitive	sensitive	powerful	joy	joyful
fulfillment	creatrix	keys	codes	downloads	frequency	vibration	manifestation	manifest(ing)	empath(ic)
spiritual	resonance	mission-driven	humanity	humane	balance	retreat, rest	bridge, bridge walker	third door	Mysticism
wisdom	shaman	moons	stars	direction	astrology	chart	map(ping)	seer	clarity
Truth	illumination	movement	amplification	simplify	multiply	wealth	prosperity	abundance	attraction
law of attraction	(Divine) Feminine leadership	soulful	soulful leadership	solo/soul-preneur	right livelihood	foundation	coherence	congruence	ancestors
dreams	weaving	exploring	co-creating	cycles	seasons	rhythms	process	allowance	desires
shape-shifter	essence	(self-) expression	embodiment	Universe	release	heal	shadow	light	darkness
aura	chakras	Reiki	channeling	Akashic Records	transmission	meditation	flow	breath	breathwork
grounding	dimension(s)	5D	3D	self	Higher Self	energetic field	sewing	reaping	harvest
expansion	contraction	growth	high	low	receive	generative	self-care	vitality	presence
empowerment	past lives	(self-) doubt	(self-) judgment	witness(ing)	freedom	safe/holding space	open	depth	facilitator
arts/artist	desire	hypnosis	trauma	archetypes	essential oils	gifts, genius	angels	family constellation	authentic(ity)

Brand Colors and Visuals

Rich jewel tones, purple, teal, gold, metallics, bright colors. Use a diverse range of images that are consistent in their textures, colors, and patterns. Include text that resonates from the heart. Make sure to use an abundance of images of yourself as well as images that evoke emotion, soul response, freedom, openness, and connection to self.

| PURPLE | COBALT BLUE | EGG YOLK | TEAL | FUCHSIA | GOLD |

Examples of the Soulfluent® Mystic Business

Mystic Example #1: L'Alchimie Sacrée
—Olivia Sautereau, Transformation Mentor

Olivia's brand L'Alchimie Sacrée exemplifies the intuitive Soulfluent® Mystic Archetype. She invites her audience to transform from within using their intuition and other Mystic tools such as astrology, Reiki, meditation, and personal desire in order to alchemize their lives and to become fully self-expressed. Her images showcase the natural world, the power of being in circle, and the restorative power of nature and meditation to support each of us in creating inner harmony and self-actualization. Olivia's use of neutral tones, lots of gold, pink accent hues, and natural settings in her branding conveys balance, peace, and vitality.

lalchimiesacree
Mantes-la-Jolie

Je suis une Alchimiste, je transforme TOUT ce qui me limite pour vivre mes désirs. Et en me transformant, j'ai conscience que je transforme le Monde. Dès que je transforme mes peurs, mes limites, mes croyances, je sais que je modifie l'ADN de l'Humanité.

Je créé des espaces sacrés pour que les Femmes prennent confiance dans leur propre Alchimie, dans leur propre Expérience de Vie. Pour qu'elles créent l'Illimité !

Ma Haute Vision est illimitée ! L'Alchimie Sacrée est l'avenir de l'Humanité où chaque personne prendre conscience & confiance de sa propre Alchimie au contact de la

47 likes
APRIL 23

Add a comment...

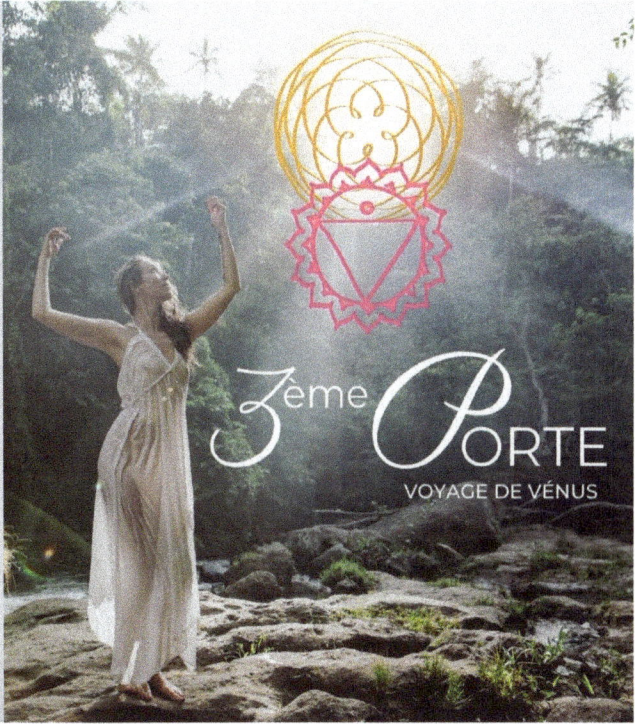

3ème **P**ORTE
VOYAGE DE VÉNUS

Incantations alchimiques 🔍

...   pour expanser mon Business

lalchimiesacree
Mantes-la-Jolie

•••

lalchimiesacree 15 affirmations alchimiques pour expanser ton Business

A réciter tous les matins en suivant précisément ces étapes. Et oui, l'Alchimie c'est sérieux !!

🔥 Choisis une musique qui te met dans la Vibe de l'Amour & de l'Audace
🔥 Met toi devant un miroir doré
🔥 Et demande-toi avec une voix grave et sensuelle

« Oh mon beau miroir, QUI est la plus belle du Royaume de (insérer le nom de votre Business) »

Puis choisis 3 de ces incantation alchimiques, à réciter en dansant :

♡ ﾐ ◁   🔖

27 likes

3 DAYS AGO

☺ Add a comment...   Post

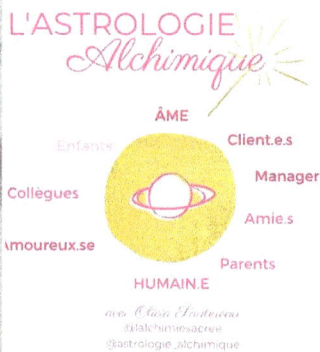

L'ASTROLOGIE *Alchimique*

MASTERMIND *Alchimique*
avec Olivia Audereau

ÂME
Enfants Client.e.s
Collègues Manager
Amoureux.se Amie.s
Parents
HUMAIN.E
avec Olivia Audereau
@lalchimiesacree
@astrologie_alchimique

3K€ par mois vs 20K€ / mois

La Transmutation Intérieure →

lalchimiesacree • Following ...

lalchimiesacree Vous voulez connaître la différence entre ces Deux Femmes ?

Le choix d'évoluer TOUS les jours et de me transformer au quotidien. Le choix de vivre ma Puissance, de l'Incarner, d'Oser vivre mes Désirs.... les plus profonds, d'Oser ÊTRE telle que je suis...

L'Évolution, la Transformation, la Puissance est devenue ma routine.

Ça a commencé avec un CHOIX, une DÉCISION,
Ça a pris forme dans la matière avec un Investissement de dingue auprès d'une coach HIGH LEVEL,
Ça s'est intégré en moi chaque semaine, chaque jour et j'ai développé

50 likes

MARCH 18

Add a comment...

Web: https://www.lalchimiesacree.fr/

Instagram @lalchimiesacree

Trademark and images shared with permission.

Mystic Example #2: BandBox Creative Studio
—Kim Charlery-Pierre, Founder and Creative Director

Kim's brand BandBoxCreative Studio exemplifies the creative Soulfluent® Mystic Archetype. Through her fashion collections and public speaking, she invites her audience to live colorfully by embracing their creative abilities and intuition and embodying full self-expression in all areas of their lives. She uses bright colors in her branding to convey the vitality of living life with passion, and as a reminder of how vibrant life can be when we are brave enough to embrace self-discovery for complete self-expression in every aspect of ourselves. Her creative expression is a catalyst for our own self-acceptance and inquiry into our true identity.

bandboxcreativestudio
St. Lucia

bandboxcreativestudio Do something different, shake things up and watch your truth come to life! #livecolourfully 😊💜

3w

bandboxcreativestudio #monday #mondaymotivation #mondaymood #motivation #motivate #inspire #inspiration #inspirationalquotes #selflove #selfcare #selfworth #selfdiscovery #selfdiscoveryjourney #blackgirlsrock #blackgirlmagic #mbib #creativemeditation #lifestyle #stlucia #motivational #motivationmonday #mentor #selfawareness #selfacceptance

62 likes

MAY 17

Add a comment...

"STEPPING OUT OF YOUR COMFORT ZONE IS WHERE TRUE SELF DISCOVERY BEGINS"

Hi, I'm Kim! I love guiding people to embrace their Creative Side by Living Colourfully.

bandboxcreativestuc • Following
St. Lucia

bandboxcreativestudio Embracing the things that make YOU truly unique is the first step toward true happiness. 😍

This LIMITED edition @dappernotes x @thebandboxofficial collection has each notebook UNIQUE by design; down to the end sheets inside!

Now available at www.thebandboxofficial.com or click the VIEW SHOP button on Instagram to get your today! #livecolourfully❣

27w

bandboxcreativestudio
#creativelifestyle
#handmadelifestyle
#handcraftednotebook

42 likes

SEPTEMBER 24, 2020

Making Art is about finding who you are and doing it on purpose!

Website: www.mybandbox.com

Instagram: @bandboxcreativestudio

Trademark and images shared with permission.

Mystic Example #3: Quinntessentials Products
—Julie Quinn, Founder

Julie is a perfect example of the ways that Soulfluent® Mystics can lead with their healing gifts. Quintessentials Products, her line of organic essential oils, invites people to heal themselves by restoring balance and harmony to their mind, body, and spirit. Her branding uses soft, soothing color tones that range across the chakras' color spectrum (from yellow to blues and purples), with gold-tone accents in the products that are both soothing and a reminder of our power to alchemize pain into harmony. Julie uses images of nature and its bounty in the form of crystals, oils, and organic matter as a reminder that we achieve harmony with ourselves by living in harmony with nature.

quinntessentialsproc • Following
Grossmont Center

quinntessentialsproducts We have
some new products!!
You can come out to Grossmont Center
in La Mesa all weekend to smell
everything!

The Tea Rose spray is a new blend of
Rose Water, Bergamot, Palo Santo,
Tulsi, and a hint of Cinnamon. It's lovely
☺
The Mask Refresh is a brilliant blend of
Black Spruce, Laurel Leaf, and
Lavender essential oils to freshen your
mask and soothe the respiratory
system!

Our new Anoint soap is a luxurious
liquid Castile soap base with organic
Geranium and Ylang Ylang essential
oils.

55 likes
NOVEMBER 21, 2020

quinntessentialsproc • Following
San Francisco, California

quinntessentialsproducts My creative approach includes balancing work, rest, and fun. Engaging all the senses is vital to my process and is accomplished through getting out into nature, out of my routine.

The joy of collaboration balanced with inward focus connects us to the creative inspiration that is always around.
#makingitsweepstakes @etsysuccess @etsy #herbalist #aromatherapist #creativeprocess #divineinspiration #healingrest #collaboration #inspired #natureinspiration #quinntessentials #organicproducts #alchemicalgold #minimalism

152w

114 likes

JUNE 5, 2018

Add a comment...

quinntessentialsproc • Following
San Francisco, California

quinntessentialsproducts My creative approach includes balancing work, rest, and fun. Engaging all the senses is vital to my process and is accomplished through getting out into nature, out of my routine.

The joy of collaboration balanced with inward focus connects us to the creative inspiration that is always around.
#makingitsweepstakes @etsysuccess @etsy #herbalist #aromatherapist #creativeprocess #divineinspiration #healingrest #collaboration #inspired #natureinspiration #quinntessentials #organicproducts #alchemicalgold #minimalism

152w

114 likes

JUNE 5, 2018

Add a comment...

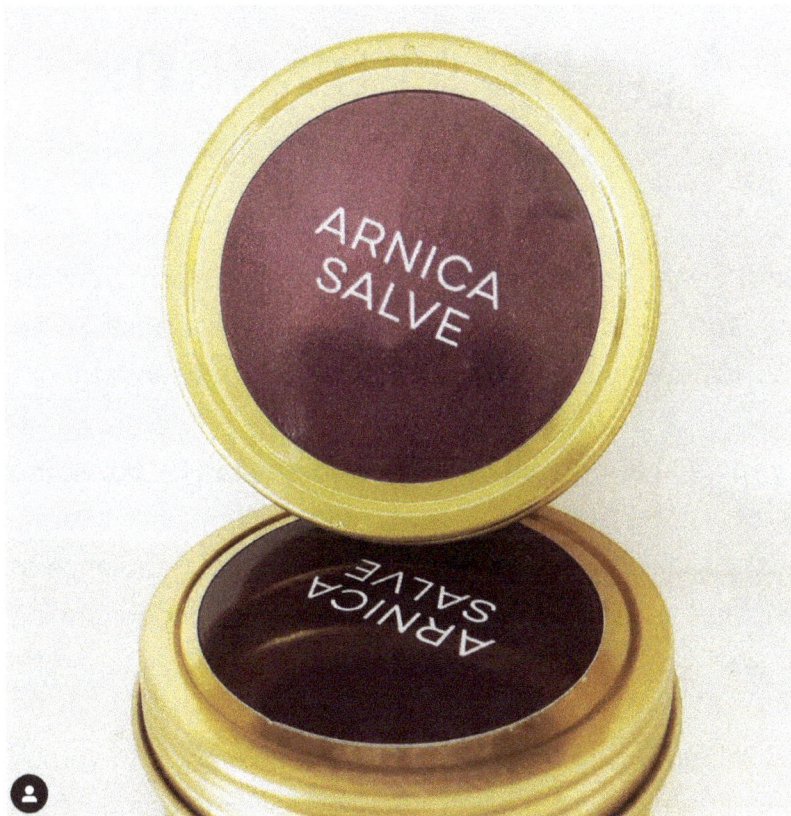

Website: www.quinntessentialsproducts.com
Instagram: @quinntessentialsproducts
Trademark and images shared with permission.

Soulfluent® Mystic Marketing

Content, Including Social Media

Focus on rich, personal storytelling. Share resonant, heartfelt experiences from your life that reveal your resilience, healing, and transformation. This models what's possible for others. Your stories can also showcase clients as well as your products and services.

One of your marketing's primary roles is to cultivate insight and healing by providing context for a person's journey. This includes sharing teachable content that informs and makes sense of specific scenarios, offering a simple framework for your audience to understand themselves better, heal, and find their way. You are the light in the fog guiding your audience where they want to go.

Create an opportunity for potential clients to experience what it's like to work with you by offering a live video, showcasing an interview with a client or colleague, and demonstrating how your process works.

You have the natural ability to simplify concepts and processes and shorten the healing time following difficult situations. You provide a safe, nonjudgmental space for **healing, growth, transformation, feeling, and believing in self, vision, and goals**. Make sure your stories communicate these qualities.

Lead Generation

While Mystics often gain business through word of mouth and referral marketing, it is important to have a clear understanding of marketing and then establish a framework for acquiring business that feels genuine, consistent, and reliable. This will prevent cycles of feast or famine going forward. Welcome the process of trial and error as you befriend marketing and business concepts to co-create your own livelihood. **Remember: Marketing is a means to help the people you genuinely want to help.**

Soulfluent® Mystic Business Model

Mystics are highly skilled in teaching, healing, facilitating, building community, holding space for highly transformational experiences, creating new bodies of work, or enhancing those already in existence. Because of your visionary talents and willingness to try new things and improve upon them, you enjoy diversity in how you deliver your work, whether you're teaching, facilitating, healing, holding space, or creating content.

Therefore, it's important that your offers and business model are flexible and incorporate multiple ways to deliver your gifts.

This way, you can showcase all of your brilliance and avoid getting bored.

Your businesses and work will evolve as *you* evolve, so stay open to expansion and pivots. Changes will serve you well, yet your work will always come down to your dominant motivation to lead: elevating consciousness and facilitating transformation through your intuitive, healing, and creative abilities.

A business model that highlights your impressive gifts and that is spacious enough to let your creative talents, interests, and abilities shine will serve you and everyone around you.

Place your intuition and innate Mystic gifts (teaching, creativity, intuition) at the forefront—the very core—of how you run your business and market yourself.

No more hiding your Mystic side!

Systems and Processes

Your zone of genius is helping others grow and heal. Therefore, building a small but mighty team to whom you delegate as much of the administrative, technical, and systems side as financially possible will create space where you can conserve your energy; serve your clients; and scale your practice, work, and vision sustainably moving forward.

Ideal Clients

Some Mystics are multi-passionate and can help and speak to a broad audience, while others work best serving a tighter client profile. The key is to identify the type of client you most enjoy working with and who gets the best results from you, and to trust your process.

Do things in a way that feels right for you at this juncture of your business. Trying to copy someone's model because it worked for them won't serve you. You are capable of finding your ideal people and identifying how you most enjoy and are best designed to help them.

Bottom line: Your clients can be as narrow or as diverse in nature as you like and as your skill set allows. They can be beginners on their healing path, more advanced, or a mixture. Trust yourself in establishing the scope of your client base.

Offer Types

The Mystic's offer types are often diverse in nature, duration, scope, and outcome.

For example, the range of offers could include: 1-on-1 client work such as individual sessions or packages; group programs including Circles, masterminds, and retreats; or outcome-based courses that help heal inner-child wounds, for example, or that teach a specific modality such as Astrology, Reiki, Akashic Records, or Hypnosis.

The Mystic's offers are centered around inner work and personal development, with the goal of a specific transformational outcome. They are deep, results-driven experiences that help others go within to find their own answers.

Soulfluent® Mystic Team Building

Who You Need on Your Team

Mystics work best with people who are highly attuned to energy and intuition (i.e., people who speak your language and understand how you operate) while also being able to complement the skill sets that you don't have.

Mystics tend toward doing everything themselves, but it's important to trust yourself to delegate and to pay for support, which allows you to trust money, trust yourself as a leader, and preserve energy for your masterful healing work.

As a Mystic, you must learn to clearly communicate the intricacies of your vision and all the components of your projects to your team members. Make sure your staff repeats what they've heard to guarantee you're all on the same page.

> **Mystics have a tendency to be impatient, so avoid unrealistic expectations by setting reasonable goals and clear timelines for tasks.**

You work well with Strategists, some Visionaries, and with Divine Feminine Archetypes (in this order):

• **The Strategist** is able to manage and implement all the details and moving parts of the bigger vision that can overburden the Mystic.

• **Visionaries** are great at inspiring the Mystic to stay focused on big ideas.

• **The Divine Feminine,** with its intuitive, organic way of operating and of inviting time off for self-care, reminds you to not overwork, to play, to trust the timing of things—and that you don't have to do everything by yourself.

Your best team members:

- Understand energy and appreciate your process.

- Are highly intuitive and offer a fresh perspective.

- Are detail-oriented and passionate about your work, are supportive, and are masterful and efficient in their skill set and delivery.

3 things for *you* to remember:	3 things for *your team* to remember:
1. It's safe and wise to have team support.	1. You will keep them focused and on track and may play "therapist" when they get overwhelmed.
2. You can afford it, and it will benefit your energy, productivity, mood, and earning potential.	2. You will keep reminding them of both the big picture and details in order to move projects forward.
3. Having support results in more time for you to help others.	3. You need your own time and process to make decisions. You cannot be pressured.

If you are working with a Mystic

Know that Mystics care very deeply about their work.

Because they can feel burdened by people's suffering and have a genuine desire or drive to help as many people as possible, **you can help them maintain solid boundaries and implement systems and processes that prevent them from over-committing and overworking themselves.**

Having kind but firm gatekeepers—along with a great customer service team—serves the Mystic well, as does having clear policies around refunds and late payments.

The Mystic can easily be pulled off track by someone else's needs or woes. When Mystics are overworked they become cranky, impatient, and prone to making mistakes. The best way for them to stay focused is through systems or individuals that can handle project management, bookkeeping, calendar management, email marketing campaigns, travel details, technological projects, and day-to-day upkeep. This will also keep the Mystic happy, well, and energized.

> **When overwhelmed, Mystics need reminders to take a breath.**
>
> **A team member who's part mega-strategist, part compassionate therapist and self-care advisor would be the perfect support for a Mystic.**

Because Mystics have their own inner processes of decision-making, strategic thinking, and research, it's critical for them to have a space in which those are trusted, honored, and protected.

It's counterproductive to try to put a Mystic into a box or a system that doesn't resonate or that's too big for them to understand, let alone manage. For Mystics, trust is very much earned, often through active listening and being able to hear in between the lines (language, tone of voice, what's not being said as much as what is being said). While Mystics can be very forgiving, broken trust is something to be avoided.

Soulfluent® Mystic Mindset

Money Consciousness

Your greatest personal edge over others *and* your greatest opportunity to achieve prosperity is the way you utilize your gifts for the greater good. Mystics don't always start off with a healthy and robust relationship to money. However, dismantling old programming around money and money beliefs will help you create healthy communion with the energy of money. Doing this belief work poises you to live a healthy life in which you can make a financial impact on causes you believe in, starting with your own business, and then moving on to other organizations and ventures.

> **Don't fall into the trap of endlessly "working on yourself" before you are ready to start making money. Share your gifts *as* you create an empowered relationship to money.**

For Mystics, the greatest opportunity for money and wealth-building is through social investing, venture capital (around which a new paradigm is emerging, by the way), and cooperative pooling of resources for community-building and impact-expansion.

Visibility Consciousness

Mystics have a very real fear of being seen. The medicine for this is taking time to familiarize yourself with your power and gifts and deciding how to use them in a way that feels supportive and safe. It is helpful to be in community with other Mystics who see the world through the same lens. Lean into your path instead of fighting it. Release old cultural and family programming and ancestral wounds that make it unsafe to be seen, heard, and paid for your innate talents. You can share your gifts safely, fulfill your desire to help others, *and* serve the greater good abundantly and sustainably with your Mystic power.

Looking outside of yourself for answers instead of within, being impatient and too hard on yourself, living in self-doubt, spinning, overworking, forcing, feeling scattered, ungrounded, and overwhelmed, Feeling bad-tempered, moody, invisible, unmotivated, unappreciated, overworked, fatigued.

Mystics are highly prone to self-doubt, which leads them to hold back from taking bold chances and from feeling safe enough to share their intuitive, healing, and creative abilities in the world.

Avoiding the Pitfalls

- **Move at your own pace as you reveal and integrate your gifts into your work.** Feeling safe is paramount to this integration, as is the willingness to be surrounded by other Mystics who understand you and who will support you in your endeavors.
- **Trust your own process and intuition.** While it is prudent to seek outside mentorship to support you, never let someone's guidance outweigh your own inner knowing, no matter how successful or knowledgeable they seem. *If it doesn't feel right, trust that, even if it makes no logical sense at the time.*
- **Start where you are (i.e., progress over perfection).** Sometimes your vision can seem really big, even overwhelming. But you can only move forward if you start somewhere—and the best "somewhere" is exactly where you are.
- **Confidence is built through action.** Taking baby steps consistently and trusting yourself and the creation process will generate enough confidence-building momentum to carry you forward.
- **Lean into your inner Mystic wisdom and especially your intuitive, healing, and creative abilities.** Focus on what comes easily to you—and yes, you can be paid really well for this.

Befriending and truly embracing your Mystic gifts can be an ongoing process. Those first steps might feel scary at first, but over time you'll be able to discern when they are aligned. After that, you can choose to step into what's next with confidence and wisdom, knowing that everything you share has value for those ready to receive it.

Mystic Mantras

When you want to reconnect to the energy of your Soulfluent® Mystic Archetype or need a boost to help you trust yourself and your way of doing things, come back to these phrases:

I need to feel into the energy before choosing my next step.

Is this in alignment?

Anything is possible.

*I am enough, my work is enough,
and I'm ready now to make a difference with my talents.*

What my clients are saying......

Soulfluent® Mystic Leader

"I knew that trusting my intuition was key for creating success in my business. And when I discovered I was the Mystic Archetype during Priscilla's Leadership Roundtable, **I became emboldened to lean in even more to my soul's guidance, to trust it and act upon it, and allow it to inform and amplify the big vision.** I'm thrilled that my Speak Shine Sell Workshop is now virtual and that my global platform is expanding. It feels so relaxing and exciting to know that magic is afoot!"

~Rebecca Massoud

Speaker Coach for Soulful Women Entrepreneurs & Creator of Speak Shine Sell

Soulfluent® Mystic Leadership Archetype at a Glance

Dominant Motivation to Lead

To elevate consciousness. To be a catalyst for transformation. To restore harmony and well-being.

Gifts

Intuitive, creative, healer, teacher, activist, truth-teller, shape-shifter, alchemist, changemaker.

Challenges

Hard on self, low self-worth and self-belief. Tries to do too much alone, over-gives, and feels misunderstood by those close to them and by the world.

Key Roles + Descriptors

Intuitive, Messenger, Oracle, Healer, Teacher, Guide.

Message	Marketing
Transformation: There is a healthier way to live life on purpose. Speaks to soul's deepest desire; preferred outcome.	Resonant Soul- and heart-led Genuine Inspired and inspiring Heartfelt storytelling

Vision, Impact, + Money

A world that works for everyone, where people see their interconnectedness and know themselves to be well and whole.

Money Consciousness: Get into the right relationship with money and the power of sacred commerce.

Business Model + Offer Types

Business Model: Scalable, personal, high-touch, allows for deep transformation. Virtual or in-person offerings that can involve travel.

Offer Types: Diverse in nature and length, focused on a specific transformational outcome. Deep, results-driven. Examples: 1:1 client work, group programs, courses, retreats, Circles, masterminds.

Based on inner work and centered on personal development. Helps others go within for their answers.

Mystic Mantra:

"Is this in alignment?"

Soulfluent® Mystic Leadership Archetype Reflection Questions

1. What does being a Mystic mean to you? How does it inform your choices, how you contribute, and how you want to *be* in the world?

2. What intuitive, healing, and creative gifts are you leading with and highlighting in your work?

3. Where can you see yourself amplifying and highlighting even more of your gifts so they are a fluid expression of your work?

4. What do you love about your Mystic talents and skills?

5. Where do you see yourself in the description of the Soulfluent® Mystic Archetype?

6. What is your next growth edge as a Mystic? Deepening your skills? Refining your process? Spreading your message further? Downloading your own body of work and process? Perhaps increasing your rates or collaborating with another?

The Soulfluent® Visionary Leadership Archetype

"I lead by creating a new normal for the world."

Overview of the Soufluent® Visionary Leader

Visionaries are truly the innovators of our species. We would still be stuck in the Stone Ages if it weren't for your audacity, courage, unshakable resolve, and willingness to do whatever it takes to bring your revolutionary ideas and outrageous impulses to life. You've been Divinely ordained to come to the planet to show us better ways of being, leading, creating, and imagining. It is indeed your role to make the vision tangible for the world to see and for your team to implement.

> **You are here to push our buttons and make us question how we live, how we do things, and how it is possible for our lives to be better, more efficient, and more vibrant.**

You are deeply resilient, patient, and willing to go where no one has gone before thanks to your resolve, clear vision, and intuitive knowing. You keep trying until you get it right. Whether the knowledge is something deep within that's been lingering for a long time or it comes as a flash of inspiration and catalyzes you to take action, you charge forward and don't stop until you've achieved your desired outcomes.

Visionaries are powerful, unstoppable leaders. They are our allies and truth seekers in creating bold new worlds and ways of doing things. Ambitious achievers who love their work, Visionaries grow companies and movements incredibly quickly and need to have a solid team and inner circle that supports them and protects their energy and time from anything that takes them away from their zone of genius.

Dominant Motivation to Lead:

To disrupt the status quo, innovate, and create more efficient systems and processes.

Gifts:

Out-of-the-box thinker, brilliant strategist, pioneer, trailblazer, highly efficient, outspoken, bold.

Challenges:

Hard on self, perfectionistic, impatient, brazen, feel the weight of the world on your shoulders.

The Soulfluent®
Visionary's Vision

Your vision is an efficient world that works for the collective good. In this vision of a better world, the old systems, institutions, and status quo that created inequality are demolished and reformed; from the ashes, new and better systems are created. In this new space, people can rise up and fulfill their purpose free from the mechanical and bureaucratic barriers that clog creativity, possibility, and the flow of life.

Soulfluent® Visionary
Manifestation Style

You manifest best when your desires and goals are as bold, out of the box, fierce, wild, and outrageous as you are. The key is never to compromise—because doing so dramatically impacts the outcome. While this is true for everyone, it's especially so for Visionaries, because you're either "all in" and "hell yes" or it's a "hard no." There is no in between.

The key to the Visionary's manifestation powers is the boldness, clarity, and swiftness of your ask. Taking too long to submit your Universal request or to act on your desire dilutes the energy of change and causes over-thinking, over-questioning, and over-researching. You then feel frustrated when you realize your first instinct was right all along.

Visionaries have an instinctive knowledge of what's right. You manifest best when you form your desire without the input of friends or colleagues. They simply may not fully understand or may try to minimize or compartmentalize the breadth, scope, and potency of your desire and end goal, unless they are deeply supportive of your Visionary brilliance or they are Visionaries themselves.

Once your goals and dreams have come into form, it's important to stay in action and then, if it feels appropriate, invite others to join you. This is a very natural process that aligns with the Visionary's love of people.

Be bold, be unapologetic, and have a blast with your manifestation style, knowing you can't get it wrong. Trust that you are the perfect person to create what you desire (and that others are likely dreaming of or will be awed by what you create). You are the one to create what you desire because others either haven't thought of it before or don't quite have the courage to see it through themselves.

Visionary Manifestation Process:

- Independently envision your goal or desire.

- Clarify it within.

- Take action yourself to get it going—only involve people who absolutely need to participate.

- Be the supervisor as you allow the project to take its own course.

- Share it with people as a way to connect, inspire, and illuminate what's possible.

Soulfluent® Visionary Branding

Brand Message

Your message is bold, polarizing, disruptive, transformational, provocative, unpleasant, perceived as harsh, truth-telling, instigative, and highly engaging. You show people what's possible and how to achieve it.

Brand Words

As you browse through the following branding words, keep in mind that it would be impossible to use all of them in your messaging and copywriting. Circle the words that you feel the most resonance with, and use these as your gauge for everything you create in your business.

Brand Words

visionary	trailblazer	out of the box	fierce	unapolo-getic	disruptive	disruptor (of patterns and systems)	possibili-ties	forward-thinking	innovative
innovation	never been done or tried before	willing-ness to fail	ability to succeed	grow(th)	change	streamline	efficiency	efficient	strategic
bold	containers	bigger vision	big	time	procedural	logical	logic	intuitive	inspired
inspiring	elevation	elevate	upgrade	results	outcome	timeless	beyond time and space	speed	accelera-tion
accelerate	fast/er	bold	loud	obnoxious	unrelenting	standing out	taking a stand	fitting in	fearless
tireless	(im)patient	outcome and results-oriented	impact	tempera-mental	irreverent	unstoppa-ble	inescap-able	impossible	possible
ingenious	lone wolf	vocal	ahead of the curve	bold vision	bold message	prosper	prosperity	profits	revenue
visibility/ visible	making a huge difference	different	resonance	brave	coura-geous	activist	activism	stirring	speak up
speak out	scary	brazen	supporter of causes and communi-ties	curious	curiosity	ongoing awaken-ing and self-discovery	transpar-ent	upfront	embolden
aware	grounded	edge(s)	extraordi-nary	ahead of the times	deter-mined	amplify	multiply	responsive	making noise
outspoken	persistent	powerful	potent	devoted	ingenuity	uncon-ventional	generous	generosity	curious
curiosity	devoted	expressive	encourag-ing	resourceful	resilient	warrior	leveraged	spacious	spacious-ness
guide	way-shower	systematic	indepen-dent	solo	system-atized	co-creative	creative	imagina-tive	scrupulous
self-trust	permission	relief	smooth/er	easier	polarizing	committed	trusting of the process	creator of new sys-tems and processes	nothing is too big or too small
open-minded	social justice, equity	new normal	better way	move-ment/ changing cultures	deter-mined	provoca-tive	dangerous	status quo	Truth-teller

Brand Colors and Visuals

Vibrant, attention-grabbing colors: red, blue, orange, yellow, all black and white, stark, rich, bold colors that are often in warm tones (instead of cool ones).

Create logos and visuals that are modern, that stand out and grab people's attention, that make people stop and think, *"Wow, what is that?"* For example, Kelly Diels (see below) uses a snake, a raven, and a spider in her branding to convey the fact that her Visionary ideas are intentionally dangerous and disruptive.

Everything about your brand and marketing DISRUPTS. Precisely because it is out of the norm, it makes people stop and think deeply about what you are throwing their way. The best way to create change through your branding is to disrupt people's habitual ways of thinking about the world and your field of expertise.

  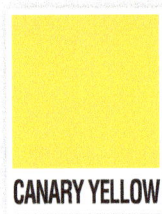   

SPICY RED   **BURNT ORANGE**   **CANARY YELLOW**   **WHITE**   **BLACK**   **COPPER**

Examples of Soulfluent® Visionary Businesses

Visionary Example #1: www.kellydiels.com
—Kelly Diels, Culture Maker, Feminist Marketing Consultant + Founder

Kelly personifies the disruptive Soulfluent® Visionary Archetype. Her homepage message tells you instantly about her movement to support entrepreneurs in making money and creating justice in a way that is equitable for all and that disavows toxic marketing practices. Her branding colors are vibrant and engaging, with imagery of the spider and dark-hued flowers serving as a reminder that she is here to be dangerous to the status quo while still very much embracing her femme energy and powers.

KELLY DIELS

☰ MENU

I'm
Kelly Diels.
I'm a
feminist marketing consultant

I help culture-making entrepreneurs & organizations bake their beliefs into their business practices. The outcome? Businesses that generate money *and* justice.

LEARN MORE

Culture Makers

We have the power to grow thriving, profitable, culture-making businesses that do it differently -- and better.

READ MORE

Hard Truth:

Mainstream marketing and **The Female Lifestyle Empowerment Brand** are blueprints for converting unearned privilege into wealth.

And they're everywhere.

The Action:

These scripts are toxic and oppressive and no damn good for us. **They're even worse for the world we're trying to create.**

Learn how to recognize the formula and its unjust business practices so **you can do it differently.**

> FLORA FIRST PRINCIPLES:
>
> **Money AND justice are non-negotiable.**

Traditional Copywriting	Feminist Copywriting
• Disempowers people by leading with pain points	• Anchors people in their power by leading with vision & shared values
• Names the client as the problem	• The client is NOT the problem
• Blames & shames the client	• Names the REAL root cause of the problem (the Villain)
• Uses SUBCONSCIOUS triggers to facilitate buying decisions	• Facilitates CONSCIOUS, explicit, informed decision-making

These days I am fucking allergic to even a sneeze of a suggestion that women are doing something wrong or need to change themselves or fix themselves *to better fit into the status quo.* **NO.** The status quo is broken. Women are not.

F*CK THE PREREQUISITES

First, they tell us, you've got to **conquer fear**

First, they tell us, you've got to **get comfortable with visibility**

First, they tell us, you've got to **feel more confident**

First, they tell us, you've got to **fix your mindset**

First, they tell us, you've got to **have a message**

kelly.diels
Chilliwack, British Columbia

kelly.diels **Confession: I'm a little tired of prerequisite-itis**

Now, some things have legitimate prerequisites. I really NEED my doctors to go to medical school, for example.

But culture making? Growing your own power? Writing? Art? Self-development? Even business...?

The best teacher & confidence-builder is experience and taking small, daily ACTION.

I used to be so scared of visibility, for example, that I had to leave my house after I published a blog post.

Liked by **emmywumedia** and **384 others**

MAY 17

Add a comment...

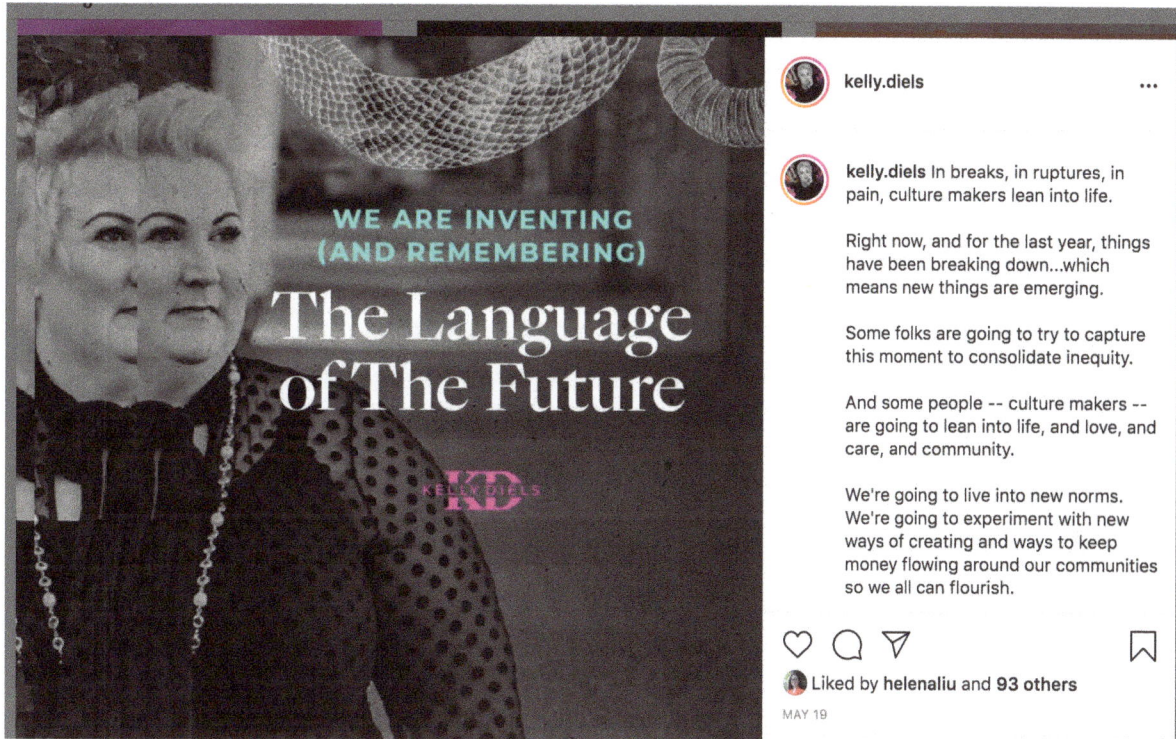

WE ARE INVENTING
(AND REMEMBERING)

The Language of The Future

kelly.diels

kelly.diels In breaks, in ruptures, in pain, culture makers lean into life.

Right now, and for the last year, things have been breaking down...which means new things are emerging.

Some folks are going to try to capture this moment to consolidate inequity.

And some people -- culture makers -- are going to lean into life, and love, and care, and community.

We're going to live into new norms. We're going to experiment with new ways of creating and ways to keep money flowing around our communities so we all can flourish.

Liked by **helenaliu** and **93 others**

MAY 19

Website: www.kellydiels.com

Instagram: @kellydiels

Trademark and images used with permission.

Miki's personal website puts her status as an innovator and disruptor front and center, showcasing her multifaceted talents. As a true Visionary, her products reveal a different (i.e., better) way to live, and a better way to think about the world and ourselves. Through her businesses, public speaking, books, and innovative products, Miki advocates for a socially just world and contributes to multiple causes, empowering others to follow their own dreams and unique path. The neutral colors of her personal brand serve as a backdrop for her disruptive message and as a canvas for creative imagery that sparks the imagination and the muse of our inner possibilities.

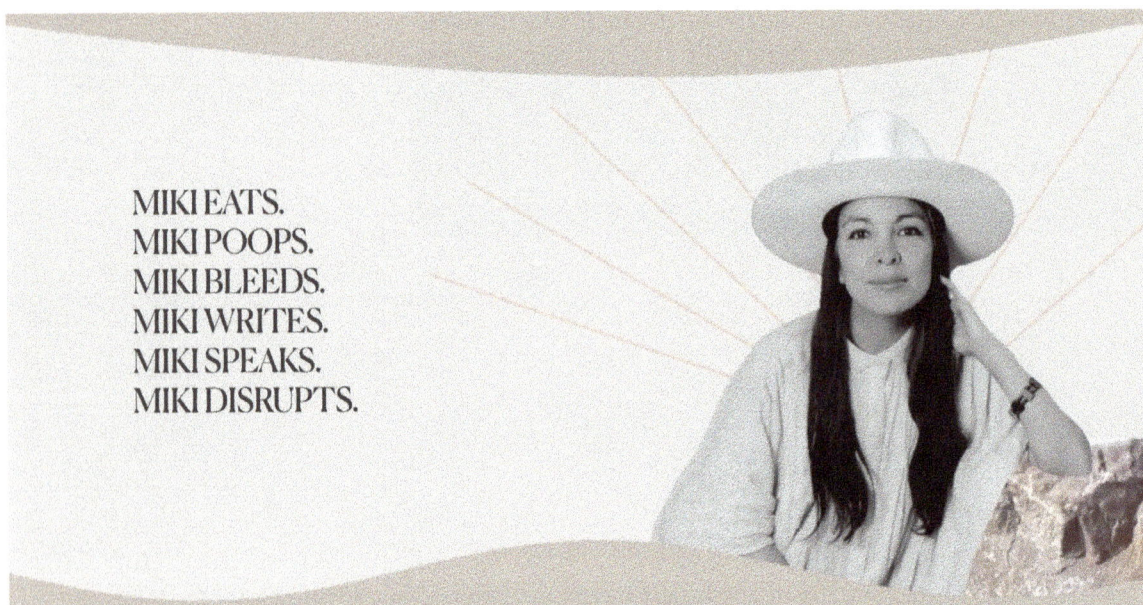

MIKI EATS.
MIKI POOPS.
MIKI BLEEDS.
MIKI WRITES.
MIKI SPEAKS.
MIKI DISRUPTS.

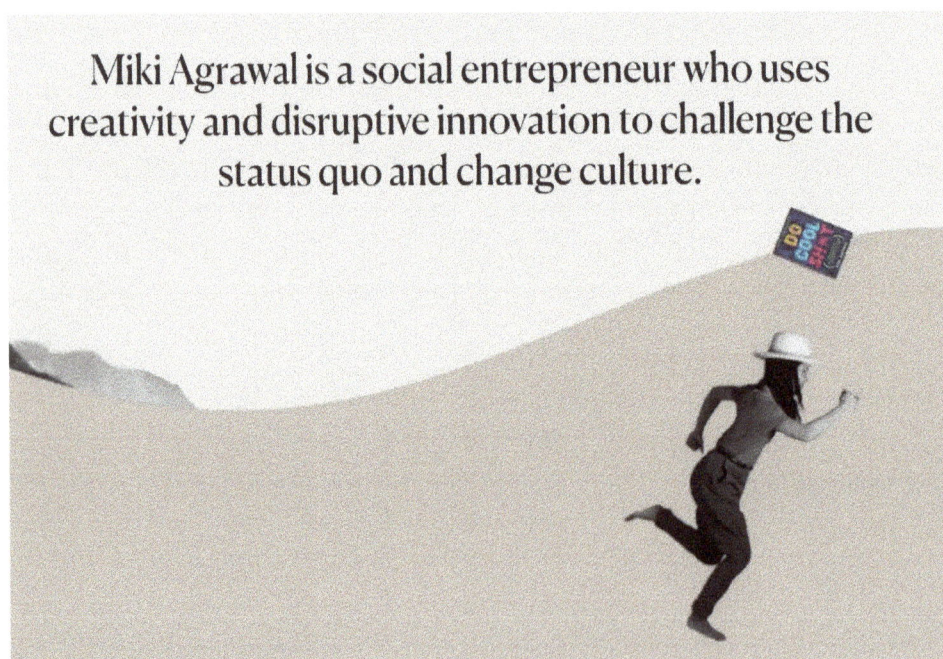

Miki Agrawal is a social entrepreneur who uses creativity and disruptive innovation to challenge the status quo and change culture.

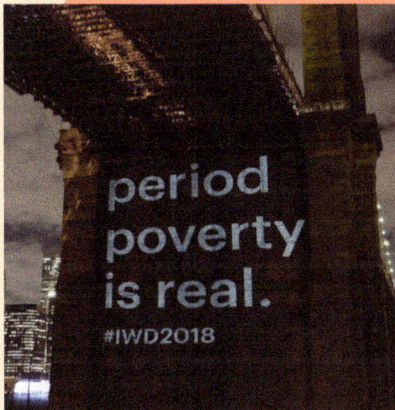

Put us on speed butt dial!

Stop wiping your butt, start washing with TUSHY.

Transform your restroom into the best room with our full line of TUSHY products.

SHOP TUSHY

Thinx •   shop   learn   mission   discover   Know Your Flow 🔴   create a Set   🔍

period poverty is real.
#IWD2018

Advocating for equity

We're pushing back against discriminatory policies, promoting inclusivity, and moving the needle on menstrual equity so that every person has access to the products they need to reach their full potential.

Today, 1 in 5 students struggle to afford period products or are unable to purchase them at all, and 84% of young people have either missed class or know someone who has missed class due to a lack of access. It's time for a change. This year, with the support of PERIOD and other members of our United for Access coalition, we're elevating menstrual equity to the presidential stage through our Thinx2020 campaign.

Thanks to you, we're able to make these initiatives possible and can continue delivering on our mission. Your Thinx underwear do more than provide you comfort and confidence — they also support initiatives that impact folks around the world. That's pretty rad, isn't it?

PURCHASE WITH PURPOSE

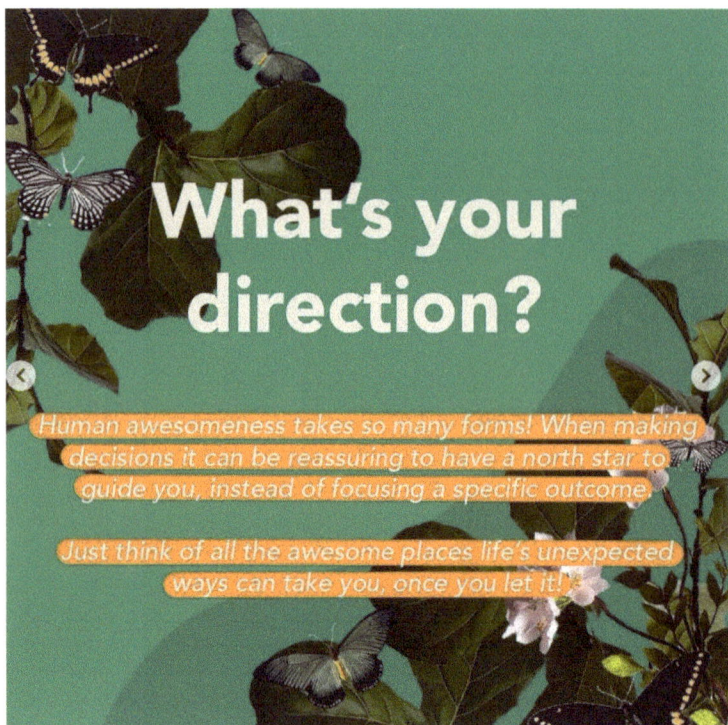

What's your direction?

Human awesomeness takes so many forms! When making decisions it can be reassuring to have a north star to guide you, instead of focusing a specific outcome.

Just think of all the awesome places life's unexpected ways can take you, once you let it!

humansarefuckinawe • Following ···

humansarefuckinawesome Calling all humans of HAFA! ☀️

Maybe having a clear sense of direction is more helpful than specific goals when life is throwing us curveballs? What do you think? Let's have a discussion about harnessing human awesomeness! 🌱

.

#humansarefuckingawesome #hafa #awesomehuman #fah #humanspirit #growthroughwhatyougothrough #collage #collageart #awesome #goodnews #love #human #positivity #spreadlove #smile #celebrate #positivevibes #inspiration #growth #selflove #learning

7w

♡ ◯ ▷   ⊟

35 likes

MARCH 13

Add a comment...   Post

Website: www.mikiagrawal.com

Instagram: @mikiagrawal @hellotushy @humansarefuckinawesome @eatdrinkwild

Trademark and images used with permission.

Visionary Example #3: EarthKind®
—Kari Warberg Block, Founder

Kari's company EarthKind® is another brilliant example of a Soulfluent® Visionary business. It not only disrupts an industry belief that toxicity is the only way to kill pests, but it highlights her movement that leads with a potent message of kindness: to ourselves, to Mother Earth, to our well-being, and to all life. Bright yet soft brand colors enrich her social media posts, which make clear that her products do a more effective job than traditional pest control methods and with less harm to the environment. Her messaging openly conveys her core values of kindness, purpose, generosity, and inclusivity—values that are woven into her company culture. Kari values her employees and her customers and gives back to her community through volunteering and contributing her time and expertise to support other conscious entrepreneurs seeking to create a better world.

earthkind.living • Follow

earthkind.living Are you looking for a way to go more 'natural' in the home? Pest control doesn't have to involve chemicals! Stay Away® pest repellents use the power of nature and are effective - guaranteed!

#earthkind #natural #nontoxic #chemicalfree #chemicalfreehome #chemicalfreeliving #essentialoils #bugs #buglife #nature #pestcontrol

41w

37 likes

JUNE 21, 2020

This or That?

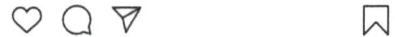

LET'S TALK RODENT CONTROL

RODENTICIDES	VS	REPELLENTS
❌ Inhumane, slow death		✅ No kill, deter mice from coming inside
❌ Attracts many animals - including squirrels, birds, and other wildlife		✅ Use a pleasant scent to keep mice out
❌ Dangerous to predators of mice		✅ Doesn't negatively affect our delicate ecosystem
❌ Poisonous to humans and pets		✅ Plant-based ingredients you can feel good about

Our Story

The EarthKind® Way Our Commitment to Social and Environmental Responsibility.

Our company is guided by a simple idea: "preserve the good, prevent the rest." We believe business has a larger role to play than delivering products or profits. Companies should take the lead to protect the health of humans, animals and the environment to create opportunities where they don't exist today.

That's our vision for EarthKind. We were first to make effective botanical pest prevention products as an alternative to poisonous pest control. It's part of our larger effort to eliminate the use of harmful chemicals in the home and in the environment.

Our mission is to reduce people's reliance on harmful pest control products from 90% today to 50% by 2025. Achieving this means empowering people with education. EarthKind is leading a movement of women and families who demand safe, sustainable alternatives. By providing naturally designed products that really work, consumers are prepared to make healthier choices. We're changing people's minds and behaviors as well as their options.

kari_warberg_block • Following ...

kari_warberg_block Living at poverty level, I never dreamed that I could make a difference, but working on our farm and witnessing the toxic, inhumane pest and rodent control methods, I knew something had to change. I discovered that 98% of all pest control products sold were toxic poisons. I knew that, surely, there had to be a safer, kinder, and yet still powerfully effective alternative out there – turns out there was, I just had to create it! I wanted to create real change, for moms like me – no matter how long it took. With determination, a relentless work ethic and an unbreakable commitment to kindness, transparency, traceability and sustainability, I paved my own way into the male-dominated, chemical and kill pest control industry – without the

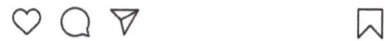

39 likes

JUNE 13, 2019

EarthKind®

Website: www.earthkind.com

Instagram: @earthkind @kariwarbergblock

Trademark and images used with permission.

Soulfluent® Visionary Marketing

Content, Including Social Media

Use visual examples such as graphs and short videos that illustrate the functionality and innovative features of what you are offering. Pull back the curtain and let the audience get a behind-the-scenes look at your process—perhaps how something was created. Be bold. Think: attention-grabbing, succinct, bold, rich colors and images. Create a big impact with less.

Go straight to the heart of the matter in your efficient, strategic, and logical manner. Use images, before-and-after case studies, and videos that actually show something in motion or what it can do (even before you've succeeded at achieving it).

Due to the boldness of what you are selling, it helps to have buy-in from the very start by demonstrating the results you can create even if people can't yet see a physical product or visualize the outcome, transformation, or process.

Explaining things in a simple, logical, and clear way is paramount.

> **Show how the parts connect and lead to the overall and overarching goal so that the person hearing your vision for the first time can understand it and see what's possible for them.**

Create your own original content as opposed to sharing others' content or any commonly accepted thoughts or phrases. Find other visionaries and disruptors and showcase their brilliance sparingly, for effect. Be consistent in disrupting the norm.

> **Disruption is the heart of your overall brand and brand promise.**

Lead Generation

Implement automated systems, funnels, and processes that allow consistent and reliable leads to come your way. Whether you choose to do launches, accept referrals, or use social media ads, have clear, automated systems in place that you can revise as needed. This way you can just press a button and watch the process unfold.

Soulfluent® Visionary Business Model

Your business model is tight, lean, super-efficient, highly profitable, and high-touch even when it's highly automated. All recurring activities should be automated, highly scalable (if you desire to reach the masses), and supportive of team-building trainings. This way, team members can focus on high-value tasks such as customer service that offer your clients a personal touch even while you run a highly systematized business. Share methodologies and tools that can be taught or licensed to the masses, that empower others—and start with your own livelihood.

Systems and Processes

Having automated funnels, detailed systems, a guide/operations manual, **a hands-off, well-oiled *automated* machine** will allow you to do what you do best and let the business run itself. In fact, efficient systems save you time, money, and energy because you are not performing repetitive tasks like client on-boarding, services, and delivery, and you still provide a high-touch experience without the day-to-day hand-holding.

Ideal Clients

Be discerning as you identify your ideal clientele, and don't budge from your vision. Understand their highest aspirations and greatest fears. Your ideal clients appreciate the good things in life, including efficiency, staying ahead of the curve, and being faster, better, and ahead of everyone else (i.e., early adopters). Give it to them and show them that their wildest dreams *are* possible—even and especially when they are stuck in stagnant, old ways of thinking and doing things.

Offer Types

Create streamlined offers that are outcome based, that make bold promises, and that align with what you are best known for. Visionaries excel with very few (often two or three) highly focused offers/ product lines that show a clear progression from one to another and that meet clients where they are at.

For example, if a Visionary's flagship program is a yearlong mastermind on how to conduct business in a socially just way, they may offer a short-term program that introduces their clients to the core elements of their philosophy; then the clients will be ready to step into the bigger program and receive the greatest benefit from it. If the company is product-based, the main offer may be an inclusive package and a downsell offer may be an introductory sampler to provide a taste experience.

The Visionary's offers are deep and powerful to the end user and provide sustainable growth and impact to the business owner herself. Their products are highly innovative and showcase a better, more efficient way to achieve their promised outcome without harming others or the environment.

Soulfluent® Visionary Team Building

Who You Need on Your Team

Because Visionaries are incredibly inspiring, it's easy to enlist people in your vision of what's possible. **You are a very fast-paced and out-of-the-box thinker and strategist.** In general, you move quickly, and you need people who can keep up with you. Having team members who can reflect back to you what you've said, summarize key concepts, and keep track of multiple projects at once is key.

Visionaries aren't great with details, although you are aware of the fundamental overarching components of what you are looking to create. You have little time and even less patience for details and should not be left to handle them, especially day-to-day tasks or spinning plates that can easily fall (for example, payment deadlines, or any kind of deadlines that have consequences). Because you are on the path of changing the world, you have incredibly high expectations of those around you.

Above all else, the people on your team need to move at a quick speed consistently (i.e., at the Visionary's speed of creation). You love the stimulation of having multiple projects in motion at once, you love people, travel, phone and virtual interactions, attending events, networking, and being right in the middle of the action. However, someone else needs to handle the preparation and follow-up and pretty much everything else that involves details. Your job is to create, to hold the vision, to be the face of your company. As one of my Visionary colleagues said, your job is to be the "show pony" or more diplomatically said, to be the face of your company and brand.

Having a highly efficient systems person is critical to keep you in flow and in motion. You also need team members who create quickly and don't mind criticism, failure, strategic thinking, or trying things in multiple ways. Above all, your team members should be more focused on getting the job done than getting credit for the work.

You have incredibly high standards of success and can be highly critical of yourself. You're likely to disapprove of anything that doesn't come close to perfection, and your team needs to know this about you.

Your best team members:

- Quickly learn, assimilate, and execute without hand-holding. They're fast learners who love a challenge.

- Handle lots of information simultaneously, make sense of it all in multiple media, and can delegate.

- Have excellent written and verbal skills, diplomacy, and attention to detail.

3 things for *you* to remember:	3 things for *your team* to remember:
1. Communicate your vision, expectations, and what matters to you very clearly.	1. You move and think exceptionally quickly, so they must keep up. They need to be excellent gatekeepers of your time and energy and hold strong boundaries with you to ensure that you don't overcommit or overextend yourself.
2. Have *excellent* detail-oriented implementers. This is non-negotiable.	2. They need to speak up and push back when goals are unrealistic—and then they need to provide alternatives.
3. Give people space to do things their way; don't micromanage.	3. They should have thick skin and thrive in a high-paced, detail-oriented, people-driven work environment.

If you are working with a Visionary

Know that they have a heart of gold and genuinely care deeply about people and about making the world a better place. However, their singular focus can mean that they come across as brash, brazen, difficult, temperamental, impatient, rude, unsympathetic, and even unrealistic.

> When you give them room to be themselves while also holding boundaries and asking them to respect your way of doing things, you'll minimize conflict and invite a greater sense of camaraderie and partnership.

Visionaries are solo practitioners and do their thing alone—often living in their minds. They want to trust people but given the stakes of what they are creating, they are often private and keep what matters most to them close to the chest. Only their inner circle really gets to know them very well. Deeply loyal, they will give the shirts off their backs. However, backstab them and you are out of their lives for good. Once certain values are violated, it's over. Visionaries are black and white and don't have room for the gray space. To them, it's a place without focus, direction, or a backbone and they don't have time to waste on such stagnant energy.

Soulfluent® Visionary Mindset

Money Consciousness

Visionaries are natural money makers who tend to have a solid relationship with money from the start, one which improves over time. If you don't love dealing with money, you recognize the importance of hiring effective money managers and a financial team to make sure you have the funds necessary to actualize your projects and to turn your big visions into reality.

Visibility Consciousness

It can be hard for you to serve as the face of your company at times, despite your passion for your inventions, creations, and innovations. You have a deep desire to fit in and to be liked (and if not, at least you'd rather not be hated). Your growth edge comes in overcoming the need to fit in and honoring your innate ability to stand out and to DISRUPT. You can be an effective steward of your visions and a great CEO as well thanks to your natural ability to inspire people, your team, and the world into new possibilities.

Potential Pitfalls

Trying to fit in, diluting your message, doubting yourself, feeling alone, isolated and disconnected from yourself and the world, overcommitting and overextending yourself, feeling resentful, unappreciated, ungrounded, feeling used, manipulated, betrayed.

Avoiding the Pitfalls

Visionaries are highly independent, which is a valuable asset but can be a stumbling block if they try to do too much on their own, thereby leading to feelings of isolation and disconnection from the world. Visionaries were born to stand out, but that's not always easy in a world that encourages blending in. And despite their love of people, past experiences of betrayal can lead Visionaries to feel wary of trusting others. As a Visionary, you will go far by being willing to heal the past and trust the person you are today with important decisions.

Tips:

- **Ask for help.** Seeking help can be a way to connect with others, show your true self, and begin receiving more support so you don't become resentful about trying to do everything yourself. Start slowly and begin creating positive affirmations to remind yourself that allowing yourself to receive is safe and feels good.

- **Build trust within yourself to share your most vulnerable parts.** It can be easy to perceive vulnerability as a liability, a weakness that can be used against you. However, as you build your own sense of safety by trusting yourself to find a small inner circle of people who have your back and who you can trust with your innermost thoughts, you will start to open up and share more of yourself with the world.

- **Build a team you can trust.** No one is an island. Given your big dreams and aspirations, you will need to be surrounded by people who excel at the tasks you aren't good at including relationship building. Be willing to trust that great people are out there who want to support you, who will not take from you or betray you. This will allow you to do your best work without feeling like you carry the entire burden of your work on your shoulders.

- **Surround yourself with like-minded Visionaries.** Trailblazers do best when they are surrounded by other disruptors who are doing great work, taking bold action, and following their instincts and amazing ideas. This is a great way to stay inspired, to keep moving forward, to feel understood and motivated. Join a mastermind of like-minded Visionaries who remind you of the impact you are creating and of how extraordinary you are.

Visionary Mantras

When you want to reconnect to the energy of your Soulfluent® Visionary Archetype or need a boost to help you trust yourself and your way of doing things, come back to these phrases:

What will it take to solve this problem?

I will figure it out.

We keep trying until we get it right.

Is there a better way to do this?

There's no time like the present to get started.

No one's done it before? Great, that means it's all mine to create.

There is no trying—there's just succeeding.

Failure isn't an option; it's an event or a phase.

There is always a way when you don't quit.

How much longer do we need to accomplish our next steps?

What hasn't someone thought of before?

It's go bold or go home.

Soulfluent® Visionary Archetype

"Since uncovering my Soulfluent® Leadership Archetypes, **I've recognized where my power comes from as a leader and how I can better lead with my team and my clients.** This has made a big difference in how I approach my business. Before I felt I was serving my clients and now I feel that I'm leading my clients and helping them understand their business instead of checking off a list of what I need to do for them."

~ *Carolynn Bottino*
Founder, Money Empowerment Project®

Soulfluent® Visionary Leadership Archetype at a Glance

Dominant Motivation to Lead

Disrupt the status quo, innovate, create more efficient systems and processes.

Gifts

Out-of-the-box thinker, brilliant strategist, trailblazer, highly efficient, outspoken, bold.

Challenges

Hard on self, perfectionistic, brazen, impatient, feels the weight of the world.

Key Roles + Descriptors

Pioneer, Efficiency Leader, Innovator.

Message	Marketing
Bold, polarizing, disruptive, transformational, provocative, unpleasant, harsh truth-telling, instigative, highly engaging. Show them how you'll create disruption.	Bold and disruptive colors; succinct and powerful messages, quotes, and videos to illustrate what's possible with processes and case studies. Clean, simple, logical (automated) funnel that's easy to rinse and repeat. Room for innovation and collaboration. Strategic partnerships and alliances.
Vision, Impact, + Money Big, out of this world. Invite people to expand what they think is possible; stretch all of our boundaries and beliefs. **Money Consciousness:** Make money and build wealth via investing, creating multiple revenue streams from innovative products, services, intellectual property, and passive income. Weather the highs/lows and sticking to the plan. Leveraging money and financial resources/funding is the key to success.	**Business Model + Offer Types** **Business Model:** Scalable, personal, high-touch, allows for incredible innovation, mass appeal, virtual, some in-person. **Offer Types:** Streamlined, outcome-based offers with bold promises that you become known for. Offers meet clients at their starting point and show a clear progression as the client evolves. Deep and powerful for the customer and creates sustainable growth and impact for the Visionary.

Visionary Mantra:

"I will figure this out."

Soulfluent® Visionary Leadership Archetype Reflection Questions

1. What does being a Visionary mean to you? What does it look like? Feel like?

2. What aspects do you love about being ahead of the curve, and which ones still feel hard to grasp and to navigate?

3. How do you reconcile your bold vision and desire to create what's not been done before (or done very differently from the norm) with wanting to fit in and/or to be liked? How has that dance been for you?

4. How do you stay brave and embodied in the vision that you have for yourself and the world?

5. What keeps you grounded and strong in your vision? Friends? Support groups? Other Visionaries?

6. What qualities do you value the most? And why? Have they changed over the years?

7. What's your next Visionary edge? Is it in your messaging? In being more outspoken and bold about what you believe in? In your pricing? In creating a brand new offer that both scares and delights you?

8. What would be next for you if you fully trusted yourself and your vision?

The
Soulfluent®
Strategist
Leadership
Archetype

"I lead by reviewing and trusting the data."

Overview of the Soulfluent® Strategist Leader

As a Strategist leader, you are incomparable and incredibly valuable. Your work truly keeps our world running by not only creating more efficient and streamlined systems and processes but by also ensuring they run smoothly and making refinements as needed.

You are a highly skilled professional who is deeply committed to causes and work you believe in. Highly intuitive and sensitive, you care deeply about the world and keeping people from suffering.

Additionally, you are highly valued in the marketplace even though you don't excel at showcasing your own brilliance. Nonetheless, your work does the talking for you. A powerful orator when required, you know how to convey a concept, idea, or thought to keep projects in motion.

You can grasp the big picture and navigate the seemingly endless sea of moving parts that are interconnected and, in the process, create solutions that are innovative, brilliant, and highly impactful for the world at large.

Dominant Motivation to Lead:

To innovate through use of reason and structure; to streamline new processes and systems that create a better world and support the greater good.

Gifts:

Detail-oriented—can see the big picture and the micro level and how to connect the dots; has the ability to simplify complex ideas and systems into digestible processes and content. Highly intuitive. Uses reason and logic, and knows how to refine and define (complex) data so it makes sense and contributes to the greater good. Creates systems and processes in pivotal areas such as science, technology, finance, law, online marketing, consulting, academia, and government. Excellent teacher.

Challenges:

Socially awkward, misunderstood, can over-rely on logic over intuition, heavily burdened by the scope and impact of your work (especially if it doesn't go right), introverted, workaholic. Has high standards for self, feels the weight of decisions, has difficulty creating boundaries, feels deeply. Dislikes or needs time getting used to being the face of the company.

The Soulfluent® Strategist's Vision

The Strategist's vision for the world is to create order, spaciousness, and flow through systems and processes that simplify highly complex data into easy-to-digest content. The work of Strategists impacts millions of people, with the vision of helping improve quality of life for every person touched by their systems. The result? More humanity, compassion, love, and possibility in the world.

Soulfluent® Strategist Manifestation Style

You are meticulous in your manifestation style and process. Careful, thoughtful, and mindful of the minutiae, you take your time to make decisions. While you are a skillful manifestor and creator, you are much more mindful and tend to focus on manifesting a few things of great importance, rather than a series of minute things that really don't mean much to you.

Strategist Manifestation Process:

- Be thoughtful and deliberate in what you desire to create and why you want it.

- Examine how that desire fits into the greater picture of your life and vision.

- Let the process simmer.

- While you are open to discussion and ensuring the decision is workable, once the decision is made, it's a done deal and you follow your own compass to actualization.

- The process is highly internalized and personal, and it can be challenging for people to dissuade you once you've made up your mind.

- Manifestation is a sacred process between you and the Divine. And while not all manifestations have to feel so "holy," you are very careful about what you choose to invite into your life in terms of experiences, people, new adventures, creations, and projects that affect your purpose, direction, and highest values.

Soulfluent® Strategist Branding

Brand Message

Life-saving systems, processes, and information are needed now to create a better world. There is no time to waste, and efficiency is key.

You are acting on your deep compassion for people and their suffering by creating innovative and life-changing solutions.

Brand Words

As you browse through the following branding words, keep in mind that it would be impossible to use all of them in your messaging and copywriting. Circle the words that you feel the most resonance with, and use these as your gauge for everything you create in your business.

details	processes	systems	procedures	policies	connecting the dots	research	data	activator	activist
catalyst	gatherer/ assembler	visionary	intuitive	numbers	information	technology	finance	academia	law
programming	time-oriented	investment of time and energy	impossible	innovative/ innovation	detail-oriented	persistent	disruptive	disruptor	forward-thinking
solo	team	delegation	team work	magic	creative	creativity	co-creative	strategy	strategist
highly technical	teacher	mentor	translator	big picture	out of the box	works like magic	derailing	debugging	unclogging
the pipeline	streamline	efficient	efficiency	noble (cause)	bigger purpose	worth the effort	hard to come by	impossible task	impossible to imagine
harder even to create	patience	transformation(al)	responsibility	solution-oriented	pathway	funnel	pieces of the puzzle	advocate	independent
precise	precision	diligent	explanation	intentional	focussed	deliberate	sensational	incredible	logic
sensitive	kind	compassionate	fierce	cares deeply	how-to	expert(ise)	guide		

Brand Colors and Visuals

Black, gray, neutral tones, lots of white space, clean, crisp. Despite the complicated nature of the issue, keep things clean or balance the dense data/content with simpler alternatives, lines, and methodologies. Use pops of color sparingly, for effect.

STEEL BLUE	MIDNIGHT	GRAY	MAUVE	KHAKI	SNOW

Examples of Soulfluent® Strategist Businesses

Strategist Example #1: NRich Digital, LLC
—Nicole Richardson, Launch and Online Marketing Strategist

Nicole exemplifies a Soulfluent® Strategist Archetype in the way she streamlines processes, connects the dots, and works with detailed systems to help her clients bring their transformational products and services to market. Her neutral branding colors (light beige, grays, and charcoal with pops of color) are typical of Strategists, who don't always find it easy to be the face of their brand, and prefer their strategies and process do the talking for them. As my personal assistant, Nicole always brings creative solutions to complicated problems, making it seem like each issue is a piece of cake to solve.

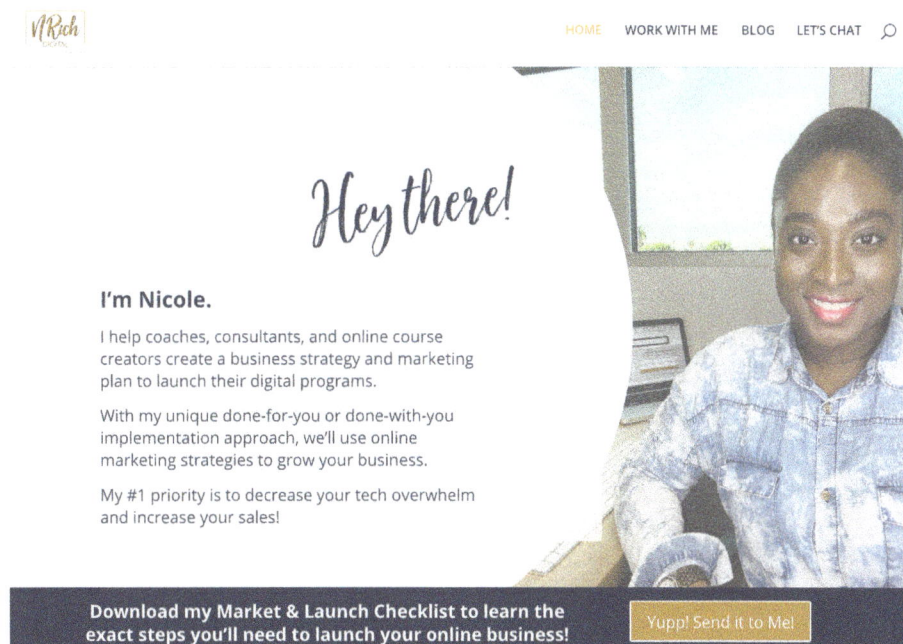

NRich   HOME   WORK WITH ME   BLOG   LET'S CHAT

Hey there!

I'm Nicole.

I help coaches, consultants, and online course creators create a business strategy and marketing plan to launch their digital programs.

With my unique done-for-you or done-with-you implementation approach, we'll use online marketing strategies to grow your business.

My #1 priority is to decrease your tech overwhelm and increase your sales!

Download my Market & Launch Checklist to learn the exact steps you'll need to launch your online business!   Yupp! Send it to Me!

ONLINE BUSINESS MARKETING:
LAUNCH STRATEGY

TECHNOLOGY

Using technology throughout this entire process is inevitable in order to put the pieces together for your launch.

SYSTEMS

Different systems are used throughout the process of creating your launch. Learn which systems will be the most beneficial for your launch.

CONTENT MARKETING

Create and distribute high-value, relevant, and consistent content that will attract and retain your defined audience.

TRAFFIC

Utilizing social media to attract attention and draw people onto your website and landing pages gives you the ability to provide more value to your audience.

WEBINAR

Webinars are powerful training tools you can use to educate, train, and market to a group of individuals that can be more efficiently done than a sales call.

EMAIL DELIVERY

Your emails will allow you to connect with your audience and give them a deeper insight into your offers and content.

SALES PAGE

The goal of your sales page should be focused and geared towards helping your potential customer feel that purchasing your offer is a no-brainer.

PURCHASE DELIVERY

In the final piece of your strategy, the purchase delivery is the most important. Deliver everything that you promised to provide to your new customers.

For more details, visit www.nrichdigital.com

3 steps
TO LAUNCH
YOUR
FUNNEL

NRich
DIGITAL

"

With anything you create, take notice at what's resonating with your audience.

NRICHDIGITAL.COM

CONTENT CURATION
Checklist
- Decide how frequently you want to post on all platforms.
- Use on brand images.
- Repurpose content you

Services 17w

#DIGITALMARKETING

Create a customized funnel experience

FREE LAUNCH CALENDAR & CHECKLIST

DOWNLOAD NOW

12 Week
LAUNCH CALENDAR & CHECKLIST
for Your Coaching Business

NTH ONE

ok

Website: www.NicoleRRichardson.com

Instagram: @nicolerich.digital

Trademark and images used with permission.

Tribal Impact® exemplifies the Soulfluent® Strategist's superpower of creating innovative, process, and data-driven solutions to large-scale problems. This UK-based brand helps companies around the world turn their entire business into a relationship growth engine via their most trusted and credible brand voice—their employees. This is a big-picture method of creating a win-win-win by reverse engineering social media strategies so you leverage your employees' natural strengths to create engagement, brand awareness, and business growth. Tribal Impact® does this across their clients' organizations through employee advocacy, social selling, digital leadership, and expert influencer activation programs. By combining precision, data-driven systems and teaching, this company connects the dots for their customers, clients, and employees—and in true Strategist fashion they're doing it by distilling complex concepts into digestible and actionable solutions that support the greater good.

Empower Your Tribe
Extend Your Impact

Turn your entire business into a relationship growth engine via your most trusted and credible brand voice - employees.

When you adopt a holistic approach to activating employees on social media you'll create conversations at scale, drive stronger influence within the market, deepen relationships with your customers so you start to attract your ideal customers, not chase after them.

Learn More >

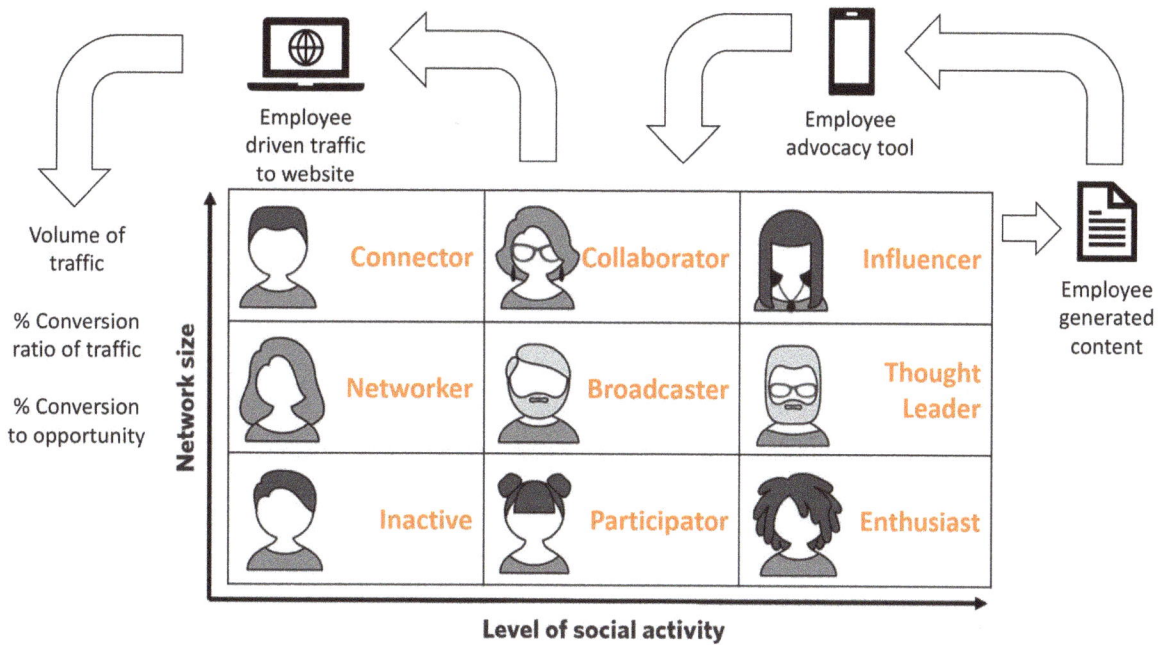

Employee driven traffic to website

Employee advocacy tool

Volume of traffic

% Conversion ratio of traffic

% Conversion to opportunity

Employee generated content

Network size

Connector	Collaborator	Influencer
Networker	Broadcaster	Thought Leader
Inactive	Participator	Enthusiast

Level of social activity

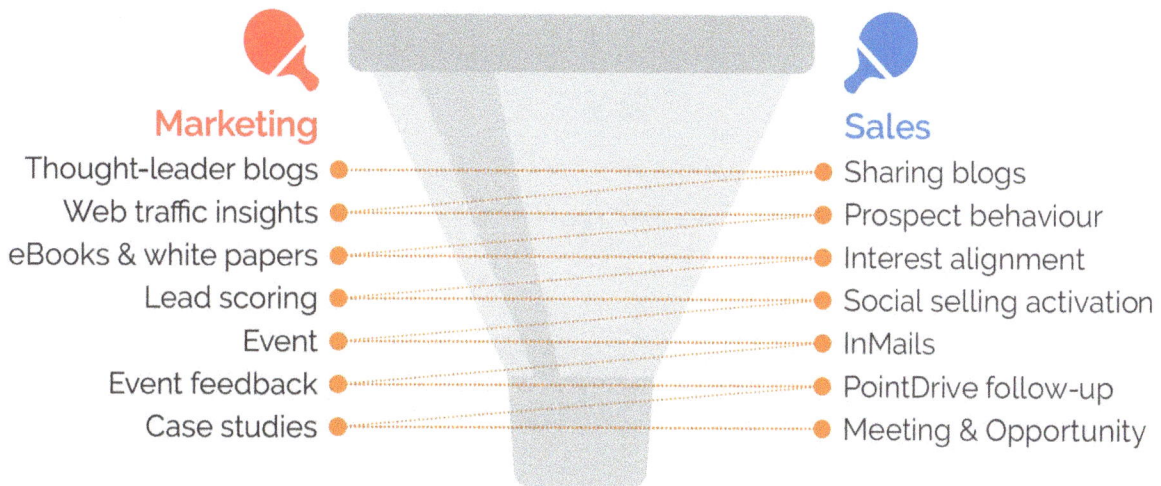

Marketing
Thought-leader blogs
Web traffic insights
eBooks & white papers
Lead scoring
Event
Event feedback
Case studies

Sales
Sharing blogs
Prospect behaviour
Interest alignment
Social selling activation
InMails
PointDrive follow-up
Meeting & Opportunity

Website: www.tribalimpact.com

Instagram: @tribalimpact @sarahgoodall

Trademark and images used with permission.

Klarinet Solutions exemplifies the Soulfluent® Strategist Archetype's commitment to streamlining complex processes and systems in innovative and creative ways that make them easy for a large audience to use. They do so by investing in customer relationships, getting to the root of digital workplace problems, and designing modern solutions that work for the organization and its users.

For Klarinet Solutions, their mission of empowering organizations to deliver a clear vision and connect employees to their work, company, and community is actualized through their focused scope of work. In their words: "We are devoted to making today's best technologies optimally efficient and easy to use." In particular, they provide their clients with clear, simple, and efficient digital workplace solutions with their SharePoint, Intranet, Office 365, and Digital Workplaces in award-winning fashion.

ABOUT KLARINET

Klarinet

[klar-uh–net]

Proper noun. 1. A provider of clear, simple and efficient digital workplace solutions, delivering what clients want and expect from their SharePoint and Office experiences. Origin: 1. From German klar "clear."

Example of use: "Klarinet revolutionized the way we do business."

Intranet Analytics

Our SharePoint analytics tool, Velocity Site Metrics, was built and engineered by expert architects at Klarinet. Equipping you with better insights than Google Analytics, Velocity allows you to analyze your intranet, gain reliable data and make constant improvements.

- **SharePoint integration**
- **Usage statistics**
- **Custom reports**
- **Heat maps**

SharePoint Managed Services

No need to stress about the day-to-day of intranet management. We act as your fully outsourced SharePoint team. We provide Office 365 and SharePoint consulting, strategy and resources that you can tap into when you need them.

- **Consulting & support**
- **System administration**
- **System monitoring**
- **Updates & patching**

Modern Workplace Consulting

We support modern workplace projects and migrations through SharePoint, Microsoft 365, Teams and other technologies, creating intranet solutions that allow employees to work smarter and faster.

- **SharePoint Intranet**
- **Office 365**
- **Teams**
- **Valo Intranet**

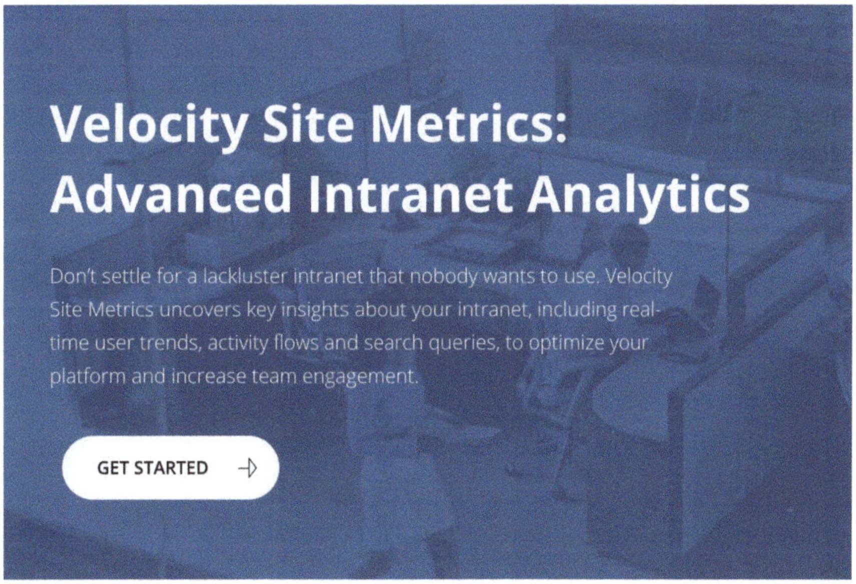

Velocity Site Metrics: Advanced Intranet Analytics

Don't settle for a lackluster intranet that nobody wants to use. Velocity Site Metrics uncovers key insights about your intranet, including real-time user trends, activity flows and search queries, to optimize your platform and increase team engagement.

GET STARTED →

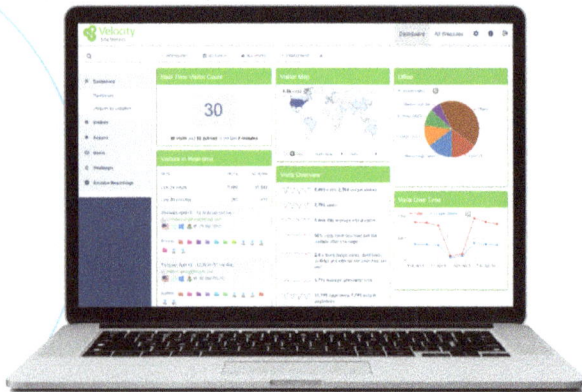

Boost Team Engagement With SharePoint Intranet Analytics

Velocity Site Metrics, built and engineered by Klarinet Solutions' expert architects, is your go-to SharePoint analytics tool. We created Velocity Site Metrics out of a desire to understand SharePoint user behavior, drive intranet improvement and promote stronger collaboration.

Klarinet

RETURN TO WORKPLACE   ABOUT US   SOLUTIONS ∨   CASE STUDIES   BLOG & NEWS ∨   CAREERS   CONTACT   866.211.8191

WHAT CAN YOU DO WITH VELOCITY SITE METRICS?

Conventional web analytics programs like Google Analytics don't offer the full picture when it comes to analyzing how users interact with your intranet and the tools they prefer. Velocity Site Metrics provides the most extensive, relevant metrics that are custom to your SharePoint intranet.

Analyze

Create custom dashboards that provide a clear view into intranet user patterns. Acquire the knowledge you need to engineer a better intranet.

- Get real-time, active visitor insights
- Measure page effectiveness with activity heatmaps and SharePoint search query metrics
- Build user segments, user flows and paths

Adapt

Leverage intranet analytics data to increase usage, collaboration and productivity. Tailor your intranet to your team's needs so you can deliver the best workplace experience possible.

- Strengthen internal communications
- Encourage ongoing feedback
- Improve file accessibility
- Revamp inefficient processes and better define actionable business goals

Engage

Reach new levels of intranet user engagement and adoption. By learning what users want, you can keep them active, interested and happy.

- Understand what's popular based on downloads and search terms
- See what news or posts are being read
- Learn how to create content users are more likely to engage with

Privacy & Cookies Policy

Managed Services

You need a variety of skill sets to manage your business apps, from architecture and design to content and data analysis. We collaborate with your existing team to enhance the work you're already doing and offer specialized expertise where it's needed.

- **System monitoring**
- **Troubleshooting**
- **Updates & patching**
- **Backups**
- **Solution architecture**
- **Administration**
- **Training**

Strategy

We set regular milestones to assess performance, review your goals, and plan the next phase of improvements to your Microsoft productivity suite.

- **Quarterly briefings**
- **Monthly webinars**
- **Annual reviews**
- **Intranet analytics software**

Consulting Hours

Flexible monthly consulting hours can be used for training, development, architectural work or projects. Unused hours roll forward to the next month, so you can leverage managed services when you need them the most.

Business Process Automation Tools Designed to Solve Tough Challenges

Do you struggle to manage complicated work processes and inefficient business apps that do more harm than good?

At Klarinet, we do the heavy lifting to build powerful business applications that engage employees, reduce mistakes and simplify complex tasks. We use Power Apps and Power Automate to implement low-code internal apps that streamline and automate repetitive processes.

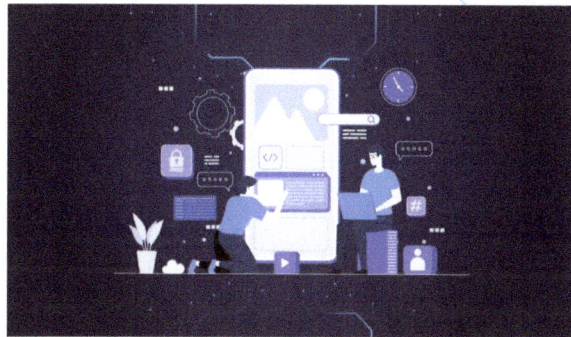

Power Apps & Power Automate Solutions

Klarinet offers two options for business process automation solutions. You can choose from our library of pre-built apps, OR submit your app requirements for a custom solution.

Financial / Legal Solutions

- Expense Reporting
- Purchase Request/Approval/Shipping
- Contract/Document Approval Process

People Solutions

- People Directory
- Photo of the Day
- Employee Anniversary

Website: www.klarinetsolutions.com

Instagram: www.instagram.com/klarinetsolutions

Trademark and images used with permission.

Soulfluent® Strategist Marketing

Content, Including Social Media

Create content that is data- and process-driven—content that illustrates how a concept or process works and benefits the customer. When possible, make your content engaging, colorful, and people-driven by showing how your work serves the end user. **Emphasize what is often underexplained or overly complex in a way that is accessible and digestible to a broader audience.** Consider having someone on your team to help translate complex concepts into simple elements, especially vis-à-vis marketing, requesting additional funding, and gaining ongoing support for a project. Keep it fresh, clean, crisp, concise, focused, and to the point, and show clearly where you are taking the audience/final user.

Lead Generation

Have clear processes and systems in place to bring in new customers. Use strategic partnerships and alliances, and enlist the right people who are willing to contribute to your work. Using your influence, get to know the key players and how to work the system to your advantage. Positioning allies who complement your work in key places is important because the "people" part isn't always your strong suit.

Soulfluent® Strategist
Business Model

Because you need to stay focused on your areas of expertise, your business is truly a collaborative affair. It's best to lean into people who have influence with funding, for example. Having team members that handle people interactions, marketing, administration, and financing is key.

As a Strategist, it is paramount to enlist ongoing support to keep the ship running as you create new systems and paradigms. You aren't well suited to carry out the innumerable aspects of your business yourself, so it's important to lean on others who are excited by your vision and who want to support it. Focusing on your genius will give you the much-needed room to do the things you do best—the things that, frankly, very few can do as well as you can.

Systems and Processes

These are critical to your success, but take your time establishing them. While creating new systems, things may get messy as you pore through information, data, and books in the process of uncovering a new way of doing things. You need space and time to lay out all the moving parts as you make sense of things, after which you'll be able to catalogue and systematize things in an intelligible way.

Ideal Clients

Your audience appreciates the technical aspects of information, and you have the gift of connecting with a broader audience who appreciates how simply you break things down. It's important to be mindful of both.

Often, the decision-makers are highly technical, skilled people who have been in your particular field for a while, so it's important to understand what you are offering as an end result, and to deliver it as exactly and as precisely as possible.

The Strategist's offers are bold, driven by processes, data, and results. They are life-changing, deeply innovative, and focused on a specific transformational outcome.

Soulfluent® Strategist Team Building

Who You Need on Your Team

Because the Strategist's work is so multifaceted, layered, and process-oriented, by nature you work as a part of a team. While you may be the visionary leading a project, you are always a part of something bigger than yourself. It's important that your team focus on the greater good as well.

You are highly skilled, and so you bear the brunt of strategic planning, strategizing, and creating the technology and methodologies that will bring innovation and new ways of doing things. Strategists are accustomed to working in teams, though you like to focus on your work and have minimal or very focused interaction with team members.

While you don't do anything for praise and make everything look easy, you are moved by your team's appreciation and recognition of the degree of effort, time, and creative thinking involved in doing this crazy, impossible work.

Strategists have very high standards for themselves, which can be transmitted to the project goals and team members. Remind your team that everyone is in it together, and that you're deeply committed and willing to do whatever the project requires. This will calm your fears of disappointing or being unable to deliver on your promises and appease your team members as well.

Your best team members:

- Are highly technical, adaptable, and able to pivot.

- Work independently and communicate well.

- Are willing to interface with world, board members, clients.

3 things for *you* to remember:	3 things for *your team* to remember:
1. You convey the bigger picture to your team. A project manager can help.	1. You are a worrier; they can help keep things light.
2. Team members are your allies, not enemies. You all matter, and you each have a role to play.	2. They can help you see the bigger picture so you can help them see details.
3. To minimize hurt feelings and wasted time, inform the team of your needs, expectations, and work style.	3. They need to know you can forget pieces of the puzzle, so they should ask questions to clearly understand the brilliance of your thought process.

If you are working with a Strategist

Know that the Strategist's mind never stops; they always live in their strategic mind, persistently trying to solve very challenging problems. They care deeply about people and the world, even if they don't care to be around people all that much. Give them space to be themselves and trust that they have a highly intuitive process that guides them to find solutions and to source out-of-the-box approaches and solutions to complex problems. They are patient teachers and, when time permits, are always willing to help simplify things for a colleague or client who needs it. Interruptions, small talk, and asking Strategists to change their schedule will cause friction and interrupt their strategic and Divine flow.

Strategists can work themselves to the bone. Remind them to rest and to take time for self-care. Lend a listening ear when they are stuck, at their wit's end, or scared. Remind them that this big work is not theirs alone to bear and they have a team they can rely on. Encourage them to socialize more for their emotional well-being, and to exercise and eat well to keep their spirits high, their energy moving, and their creative juices flowing.

Soulfluent® Strategist Mindset

Money Consciousness

You are connected to money through your awareness that money is required to fund your projects and that it makes the world go around. You don't personally or particularly care about money but do know it can impact the lives of many who could use your innovations to live a healthier, happier, safer life. For this reason, you don't pursue endeavors for money alone, though your brilliance innately affords you the ability to create and to accumulate and multiply wealth if you so choose.

It's important to have trusted financial advisors and caretakers in your business, as you can tend to avoid your riches or delay applying healthy habits that will allow your money to grow in positive and useful ways.

Visibility Consciousness

Most Strategists prefer to stay behind the scenes and for this reason don't make the best CEOs. That said, you are aware that you need to be visible when a launch is imminent and when publicity is required to market and share your work with as many people as possible.

When you overcome the fear of being misunderstood by the general public and are willing to find peace with your public persona, you will create greater inner harmony and spaciousness in your life and overall well-being.

Strategists can be doubtful of the next steps and their own process, and can feel lost, misunderstood, unappreciated, rushed, isolated, or criticized. They can try to appease others by taking suggestions even when it's clear they won't work and will reflect poorly on you.

Avoiding the Pitfalls

Strategists are prone to taking on too much pressure and responsibility from their clients and teammates, causing them to dislike their work, doubt their process, and overthink their next steps.

Tips:

- **Make your expectations clear.** Learn to manage your team members' and clients' expectations up front so you don't have to bear the weight of the responsibilities all on your shoulders.
- **Be clear with your clients and team members.** Let them know you have your process and that, even in a world that craves instant gratification, being rushed will negatively impact your results.
- **Be prepared for pushback.** Because you provide creative solutions to mainstream problems, you may encounter pushback that can derail your critical thinking and confidence. It's best to remind those you work with that this is what makes you so valuable (and why they likely hired you) and they should give you room to create in your way before they provide feedback.
- **Be selective about who you work with.** Choose team members and clients who can appreciate you and your creative and intuitive process, who are respectful of your time frames and deadlines, and who take responsibility for their results versus putting all the pressure on you to fix things for them.
- **Don't forget the fun.** Including light-hearted, supportive, and kind people in your life will allow you to do more and to have more perspective when life and work in particular feel too challenging.

When you find yourself feeling overwhelmed, remember to trust your instincts, take a step back and get some fresh air, reach out to a friend for advice, and know you'll get through it.

Strategist Mantras

When you want to reconnect to the energy of your Soulfluent® Strategist Archetype or need a boost to help you trust yourself and your way of doing things, come back to these phrases:

I lead by questioning the status quo.

I lead by challenging assumptions to encourage differentiating points of view.

I lead by reflection and examination of a problem through many lenses to take decisive action.

I lead with patience, courage, and an open mind.

I lead by taking big-picture ideas and turning them into bite-size tangible concepts.

Strategist Questions:

Is this the best-quality information we have?

Is there more research that can be done?

Have we tested the data?

Who else can help us?

How do these pieces fit together?

What else haven't I thought of yet?

What are some of the best (and worst) practices to consider and to avoid?

How long will this take?

Can we accomplish this on time?

What are the consequences if we do or we don't?

Let's try it one more time just to be sure: let's double-check the fine print and make sure the systems are ready and there are no major glitches.

What my clients are saying...

Soulfluent® Strategist Archetype

"I used to believe Leadership was HOW you told people what to do. And that you could either be a jerk, or be kind. Most examples I had were closer to the "jerk" archetype so I have steered clear of stepping into anything that resembled leadership.

Even owning a business, I downplayed being the boss because I never wanted to be associated as "The Bad Guy". The Soulfluent® framework has given me a completely new perspective on leadership and helped me understand that leadership is how you show up in the world, whether you are "in charge" or "just an employee". Learning that I am a Strategist Archetype has clued me in to gifts that I have been ignoring and downplaying for years.

Leaning into the Strategist is allowing me to make better decisions for my business, is helping me recognize what to delegate and I'm now able to balance the big vision with the finer details instead of getting lost in one or the other.

I'm grateful to be able to lean on the Strategist Archetype as I continue to grow into my capacities as a Leader."

~ *Heather Rangel*
Life + Business Strategist

The Soulfluent® Strategist Leadership Archetype at a Glance

Dominant Motivation to Lead

To streamline new processes and systems that create a better world that supports the greater good.

Gifts

Precise, detail-oriented, persistent, innovative, data and process-driven. Creative, visionary, diligent, highly intuitive, great teacher.

Challenges

Socially awkward, misunderstood, can over-rely on logic over reason, heavily burdened by the scope and impact of your work (especially if it doesn't go right at first).

Key Roles + Descriptors

Creator, Visionary. Precise, devoted, diligent, detail-oriented, process- and data-driven.

Message	Marketing
Life-saving systems, processes, and information are needed now to create a better world. There is no time to waste, and efficiency is critical. You create innovative and life-changing solutions for people and their suffering.	Efficiency; data, research and impact-driven; made for the masses. Simple explanations and translation of core use, application, and benefits; how it's different and how it works.

Vision, Impact, + Money

An efficient and just world that works for everyone. Greater healing, interconnectedness, and respect and reverence for science, data, and the creative/innovative process. We each have a role and are a part of the bigger picture.

Money Consciousness: Create harmony with money by seeing it as an ally and getting help to manage it. Once you create a healthy relationship with it, you may have fun using money as a tool to multiply and as a force for good—without having to micromanage it.

Business Model + Offer Types

Business Model: Scalable, personal, high-touch, high-tech business model allows for deep transformation and improvement of life. Made for and applicable to the masses.

Offer Types: Bold; results-, data-, and process-driven, deeply innovative and focused on a specific transformational outcome or solution.

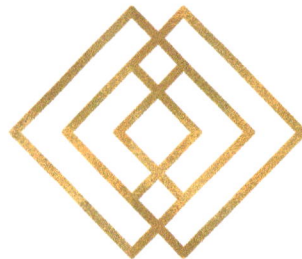

STRATEGIST MANTRA:

How do these pieces fit together?

What else haven't I thought of yet?

The Soulfluent® Strategist Leadership Reflection Questions

1. What does being a Strategist Leader mean to you?

2. If visibility doesn't come easily to you, how can you think of it in a new light that frames it around the good you are doing in the world?

3. What's your natural flow and method of navigating both the big picture and small picture (i.e., the details)?

4. What do you like about being a Strategist?

5. When you feel the burden of your work on your shoulders, how do you decompress and find perspective?

6. What's your vision for the world, and how do you keep it alive in your day-to-day life?

7. What do you do for fun?

The Soulfluent® Explorer Leadership Archetype

"I lead through experimentation and adventure."

Overview of the Soulfluent® Explorer Leader

Curious about the world, human experiences, and stories, you love to invite people into new possibilities, catalyze new ideas, connect incredible people—and are very generous with your resources. You have a huge heart, which needs to be carefully guarded so people don't take advantage of your generosity of resources and spirit.

Explorers are highly attuned. They are not naive about the world's problems or what it will take to solve them—and are often misunderstood. Your frequency is one of possibility and positivity, which is a fun, lighthearted way to go about creating change. You bring a breath of fresh air, especially in the presence of stale or stagnant energy. You make fantastic guides, seekers, teachers, and are innate explorers, and you keep everyone sharp and on our toes, keenly questioning everything we think we know to be true. While others can't tie you down, you design your life, business, and home in a way that's rooted and gives you ample freedom to travel, to get up and go at the drop of a hat if that's what calls to you.

As leaders, Explorers are natural inspirers and connectors and are needed to seed, catalyze, and evoke new ideas and possibilities from those whose lives you touch. You ask the questions that can change worlds. You appreciate trying new things, refining things until something is right, and then getting feedback. This is one of your superpowers, since you don't get offended or put off when something doesn't work. You consistently refine to make sure things are absolutely right.

The Soulfluent® Explorer's Vision

The Explorer's vision for the world is for people to realize, understand, and integrate their fullest potential. You want people and the world to recognize the magnificence that you see in each and every individual who walks the planet. From this lens of awe and possibility, you believe that people will be empowered and confident to follow their dreams, to take risks, and to create new experiences, products, services, and connections that will make the world a happier and better place.

Soulfluent® Explorer Manifestation Style

You manifest best when you feel free to be yourself and when you have the spaciousness, support, and inspiration to dream up something big and then pull the trigger on it. You never lack ideas, dreams, or possibilities to imagine, explore, and actualize—and in fact, you're a catalyst. However, when you learn to make space for the manifestations that are ripe to be created now, you will experience more possibility, joy, and freedom in the process. You enjoy your manifestations when you are allowed to savor them to the fullest. You will never create like others do; you must have curiosity, freedom, richness, and, of course, the ability to enjoy the act of creation, plan it, and experience it in your own out-of-the-box way. And, more often than not, while some of your desires are intimate and sacred, what you desire feels even richer or more opulent, indulgent, or adventurous when shared with others.

Explorers manifest as you lead your lives: experientially. When you get inspired by a thought that lights the match of desire, you go straight into research and execution mode. You work best when you seek support from the Universe and with the minutiae and details you don't love, and then share the experience of creating and experiencing it with people whose company you enjoy. The world loves Explorers because you remind us that we can create anything we desire at any time—and even have a wonderful time doing it all.

Explorer Manifestation Process:

- A spark is lit (through a person, thought, or experience).

- Enter into major imagination, exploration, and research mode to get the creation process rolling (this is not a long process—a few weeks at the very most).

- Refine your timeline of when to create.

- Go create.

- Invite others to share in the experience with you (because the more people there are to experience the process with, the better).

Soulfluent® Explorer Branding

Brand Message

"What's my next adventure?"

Brand Words

As you browse through the following branding words, keep in mind that it would be impossible to use all of them in your messaging and copywriting. Circle the words that you feel the most resonance with, and use these as your gauge for everything you create in your business.

explorer	adventurer	dreamer	dream	ally	possi-bilities seeker	catalyst	innovator	trailblazer	freedom-seeker
truth-teller	strategic	strategist	imagina-tive	curious	curiosity	dream weaver	magic maker	supporter	empower-ment
inspiration	mission	purpose	big vision	greater dream	influence	impact	income	wealth	high-quality
low-cost	ingenious	ingenuity	innovative	unstoppa-ble	resilient	persistent	refinement	refiner	willing to experi-ment
try again	willing to fail	goal is to keep exploring	asking questions	befriend-ing the unknown	looking within	experi-ences	experien-tial	people	networking
people-lover	big heart	cares deeply	multi-passionate	multi-faceted	take a stand	big picture thinking/ thinker	logical thinker	organizer	commu-nity-builder
gatherer	enroller	inspirer	catalyst	connec-tors	visionary	joy-seeker	light-hearted	fun	life of the party
values-driven	inspiration	travelers (of the world and your imagina-tions)	gypsy hearts	family-oriented	strong personal-ities and sense of self and values	enroll others with ease into possi-bilities	visions and opportuni-ties	enthusi-astic	excited and exciting

infectious	positivity	see the bright side of things	deeply spiritual	believe in something bigger themselves	highly intuitive	intuition	deeper sensing and knowing ("I don't know how I know, I just know")	"I just know"	perspectives and ways of being
open to multiple opportunities	courageous	courage	no formulas, no boxes, no "one way"	highly flexible and adaptable yet know your non-negotiables and what you like	out-of-the box creators and doers	connector	experimenter	expansive	freedom

Brand Colors and Visuals

Bold, colorful, inviting, inspiring, emotion-evoking colors. Use lots of images of nature, of places and spaces and experiences that move you, inspire you, and touch you and that you want to share with your audience.

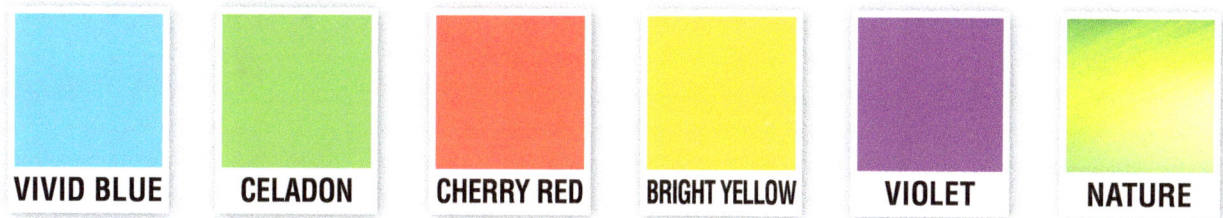

VIVID BLUE **CELADON** **CHERRY RED** **BRIGHT YELLOW** **VIOLET** **NATURE**

Examples of Soulfluent® Explorer Businesses

Explorer Example #1: The Dream Academy
—Jacqueline Boone, Founder + CEO

The Dream Academy, created by my colleague Jacqueline Boone, personifies the dreamer in all of us—the quintessential quality of the Soulfluent® Explorer Archetype. Her use of gorgeous nature photography evokes the feelings of expansion, possibility, and adventure that so personify the Soulfluent® Explorer. Jacqueline's content and website copy activate our imagination to dream big, to go for what we truly want by connecting to our most intimate desires. Her courses, retreats, and consulting work invite us to live experientially, which is how Explorers lead best: by connecting to the world, trying things out, tweaking as they go along, and making amazing new friends in the process.

WE ARE BORN DREAMERS.

A BETTER WORLD BEGINS WITH BIGGER DREAMS

We have a simple proven approach to help you identify and realize your Dreams.

Step 1: Connect to *your* Dream
Step 2: Give you tools, support, and community to help make your Dream a reality
Step 3: Take guided action

Every person is unique, so although we have a process, each Dream is extraordinary. That's why we encourage you to choose the path that works best for you.

"DON'T LET SMALL MINDS CONVINCE YOU THAT YOUR DREAMS ARE TOO BIG."

— UNKNOWN

WHAT TYPE OF
DREAMER ARE YOU?

ENTREPRENEUR

Whether this is your first company or you're a seasoned pro, you're a creator who wants to build or grow a business.

[THAT'S ME]

SIDE HUSTLER

By day, you work a 9 to 5. By night, you're a Dreamer working hard to make your passions a reality. Both are possible. We'll show you how.

[THAT'S ME]

PROFESSIONAL

Dream jobs do exist! We know because we've had them and helped recruiters hire top talent. Find the right job and career that aligns with you.

[THAT'S ME]

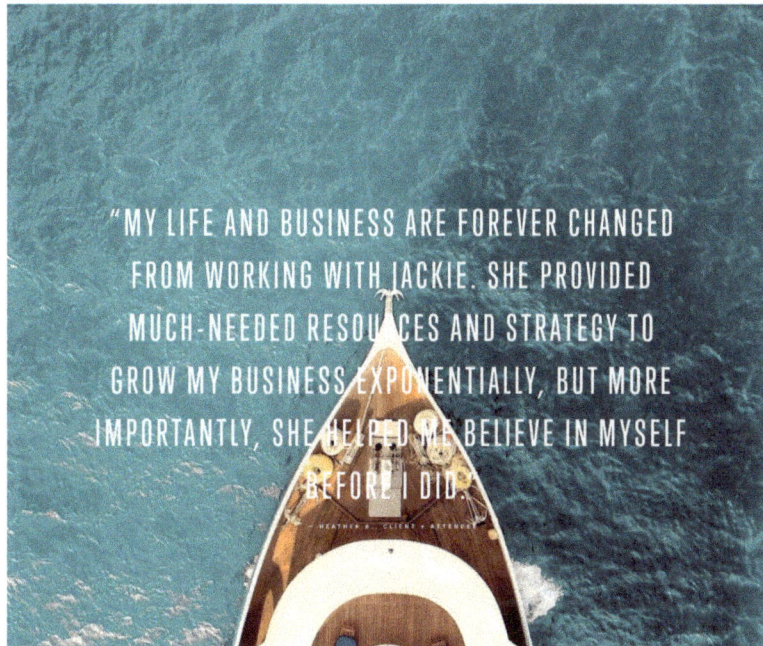

"MY LIFE AND BUSINESS ARE FOREVER CHANGED FROM WORKING WITH JACKIE. SHE PROVIDED MUCH-NEEDED RESOURCES AND STRATEGY TO GROW MY BUSINESS EXPONENTIALLY, BUT MORE IMPORTANTLY, SHE HELPED ME BELIEVE IN MYSELF BEFORE I DID."

HEATHER B., CLIENT + AUTHOR

SELF-PACED

Want to navigate solo?

We offer a variety of workshops designed by experts from all over the world, created so that you can attend from anywhere in the world. Sign up for LIVE and self-paced workshops and events that work best for you and your schedule.

SEE ALL EVENTS

THE DREAM ACADEMY

Want community and structure?

The Academy curriculum begins with the core **101 Course**. From there, you will learn ways to make your Mission, Message, and Movement ready for the world as an Entrepreneur, Side Hustler, or Professional.

START HERE

CONSULTING

Want one-on-one guidance?

We work with individuals and businesses — everyone from startups to Fortune 100 and 500 companies on creating and implementing digital marketing, business, and professional development strategies to help you succeed at work.

TELL ME MORE!

> "I COULDN'T LET ANOTHER DAY PASS BEFORE WRITING TO SHARE HOW MUCH WE ENJOYED THE TRAINING. SHE WAS TRULY INCREDIBLE!"
>
> — KATHERINE B., ATTENDEE

the.dream.academy ···

the.dream.academy WHAT IF ☀ One of the most powerful and magical phrases in the English language. That one phrase can open up possibilities we never even considered or shut us down with worst-case scenarios. Ultimately, it's a choice. What do you choose? Where can your "what if's" take you today? 💁

#dreambigger #whatif #dreams #foodforthought #adventure #explore

6w

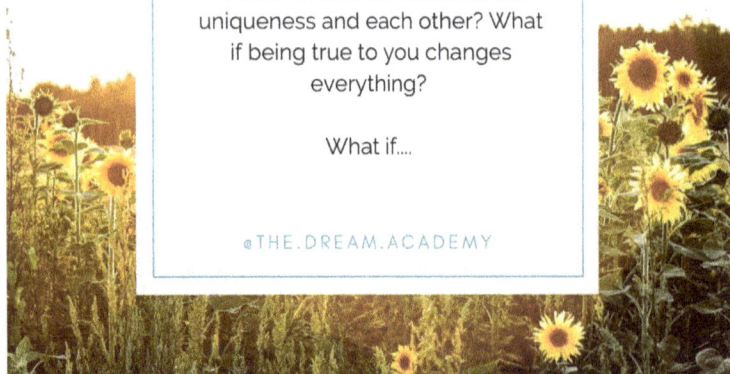

What if?

Your Dreams could create a better world? What if we honored our uniqueness and each other? What if being true to you changes everything?

What if....

@THE.DREAM.ACADEMY

♡ ⬡ ◁   ⊏⊐

Liked by **jacqueline.e.boone** and **14 others**

APRIL 7

UPCOMING EVENTS!

NOW OFFERING

A+ ACCOUNTABILITY
June 11th | 1:00PM-2:00PM EST

BUSINESS 101
June 15th | 11:00AM-12:30PM EST

POWER OF CONNECTING
June 17th | 11:00AM-12:30PM EST

HEART LANGUAGE
June 22nd | 11:00AM-12:30PM EST

101 COURSE
July 7th-July 28th | 1:00PM-2:00PM EST

CAREER CONVOS
July 9th | 11:00AM-12:00PM EST

SUSTAINABILITY SECRETS
July 23nd | 11:00AM-12:00PM EST

in ◎ #DREAMBIGGER · THE DREAM ACADEMY

THE DREAM ACADEMY

Because I Can

A SUMMER SERIES CELEBRATING POSSIBILITIES!

KICK-OFF JUNE 11 1-2PM EST

FEATURED SPEAKERS

CAROLINE NIXON · JASMINE ADAMS · MADELEINE WISECUP · DANA RAGAN

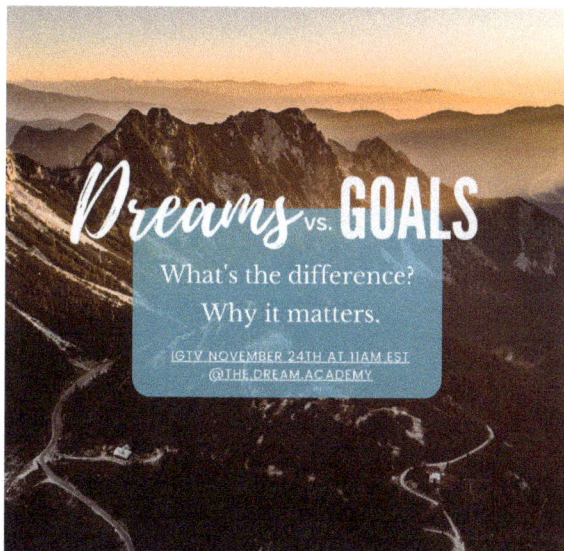

Dreams vs. **GOALS**

What's the difference?
Why it matters.

IGTV NOVEMBER 24TH AT 11AM EST
@THE.DREAM.ACADEMY

◎ #DREAMBIGGER · THE DREAM ACADEMY

DREAMER'S DAILY CHECKLIST ✓

- START THE DAY RIGHT
- SMILE AND LAUGH AS OFTEN AS POSSILBE
- TAKE ONE ACTION ON MY DREAMS!
- BE IN THE PRESENT
- DO ONE THING THAT SCARES YOU
- SUPPORT SOMEONE
- SING, DANCE, OR BOTH!
- DO AT LEAST ONE THING I LOVE TO DO!
- MAKE THE MOST OF YOUR DAY!
- *LIVE!*

THE DREAM ACADEMY

Website: www.thedream.academy
Instagram: @the.dream.academy
Trademark and images shared with permission.

Cairn Leadership Strategies epitomizes the adventurous spirit of the Soulfluent® Explorer Archetype by inviting their clients to develop their leadership skills through "gritty outdoor weekend adventures, rigorous applied study and action-based coaching subscriptions for leaders." By capitalizing on the Soulfluent® Explorer trait of learning experientially, clients are challenged to push their limits, which allows them to not only build genuine connections with their fellow adventurers but also to deepen their self-confidence and resilience. I love their belief that "Challenge makes life an adventure. Adventure makes great leaders."

Explore. Connect. Excel.

A community of intentional leaders pursuing excellence through gritty outdoor adventures and rigorous applied study.

Great leadership doesn't just happen. It takes intention, discipline, and constant learning. Unfortunately, most options for developing leadership involve boring lectures, more Zoom, and contrived games or activities.

We are the opposite.

cairnleadership
Joshua Tree National Park

cairnleadership These women all pushed way past the point they thought they would reach this weekend on our Joshua Tree Crux Adventure. Humbled, grateful and stoked to be in community with so many awesome leaders and people. Challenge makes life an adventure. Adventure makes great leaders. Go explore.
.
.
.
#cruxsociety #adventurewithpurpose #cairnleadership #leadershipexcellence #optoutside #adventure #outdoors @ruckpack @the.active.life.company @fjallraven_na @outdoorresearch @liveclimbrepeat @aacsandiego

52 likes
MARCH 8

☺ Add a comment...   Post

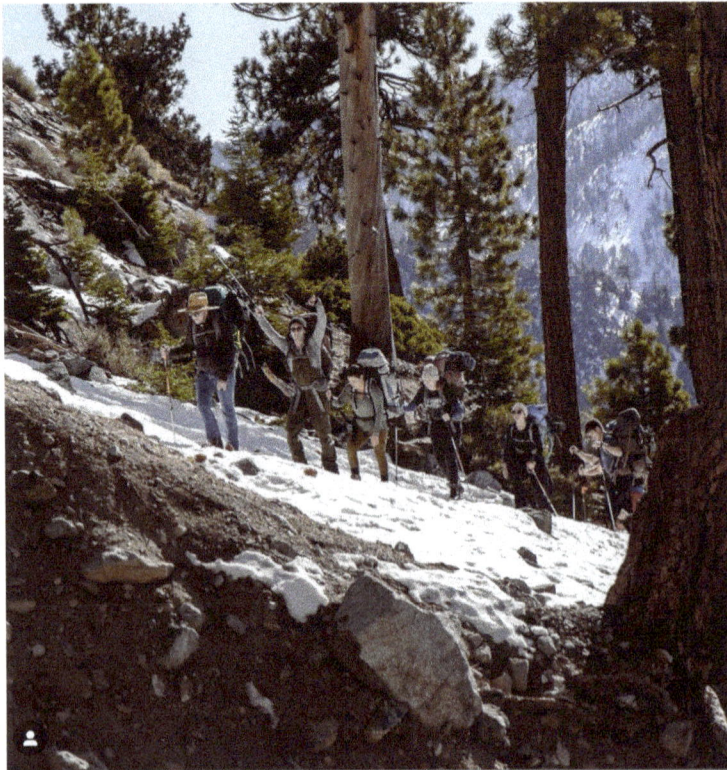

cairnleadership
Mount Baldy, California

cairnleadership Life changing... we hear that a lot on and after Crux Adventures. It's not without a little nail biting that we watch our community members uproot, make big moves, change to careers they love, give up old habits and radically confront the challenges and dreams they never thought they would. Then again all our work comes with a little nail biting as we confront unpredictable weather, rugged mountains, real risk and deep fears as a team in Crux Society, so what the hell. Dream on!
.
.
See what Crux Adventures are about and what's it's like being a member of Crux Society - Links in bio!

32 likes
SEPTEMBER 15, 2020

☺ Add a comment...   Post

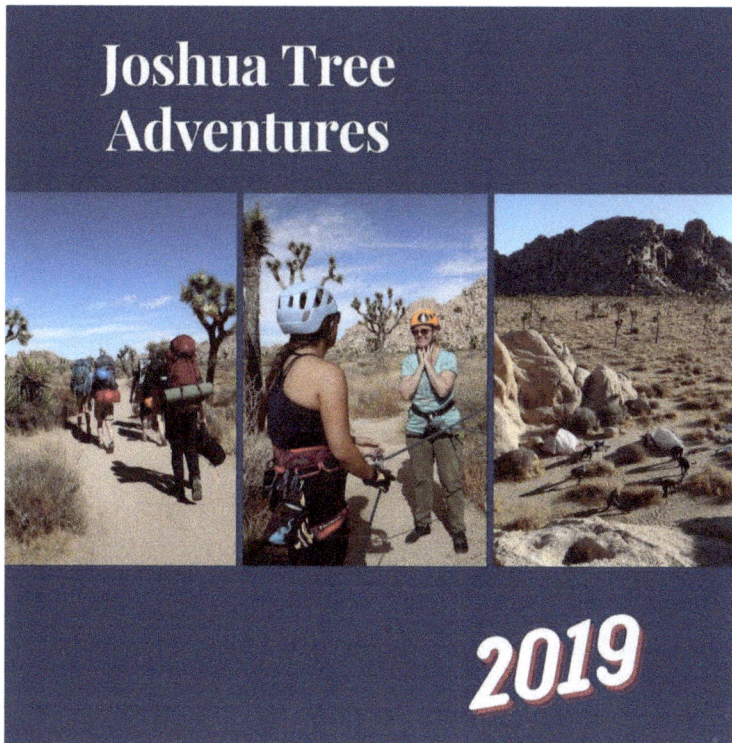

Joshua Tree Adventures

2019

---

cairnleadership
Joshua Tree National Park

cairnleadership Happy Monday! We're reminiscing on our Crux Adventure from last year at Joshua Tree. We love capturing our #leaders being in community, out of their comfort zones and gaining #leadershipskills. We have an upcoming Joshua Tree Crux Adventure on October 16th-18th and we would love to see you all there. Learn more about this trip by signing up for the adventure brief. Link in bio!
.
.
#adventurewithapurpose #cairnleadership #leadershipexcellence #optoutside #adventure #outdoors

@ruckpack @the.active.life.company
@tideline.coffee

9 likes
SEPTEMBER 14, 2020

Add a comment...

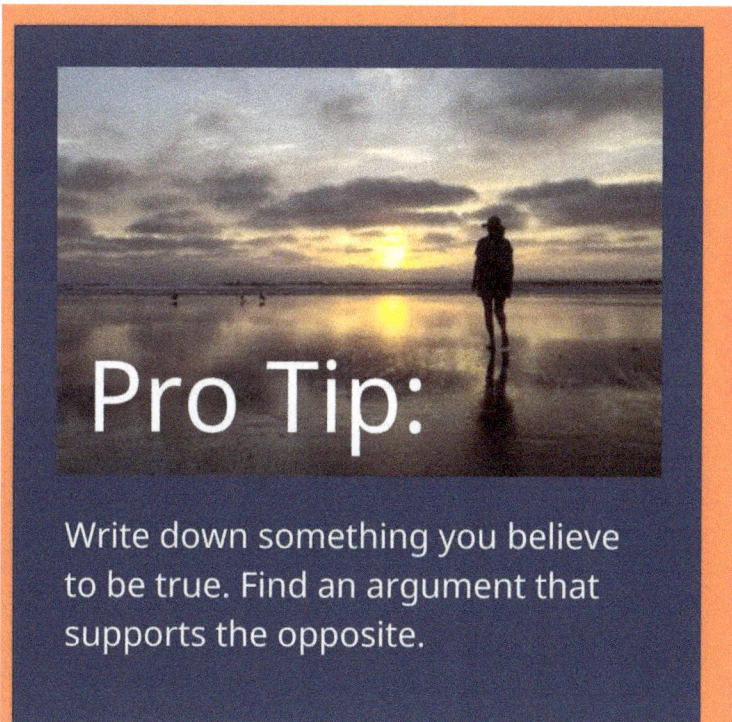

Pro Tip:

Write down something you believe to be true. Find an argument that supports the opposite.

---

cairnleadership
San Diego, California

cairnleadership Learn more about #criticalthinking #problemsolving and #strategic skills as a #leader with our sixth leadership competency. Work on these skills with us on an adventure or on a leadership coaching session with us! Checkout our bio for links to our upcoming adventures, leadership competency modules and our #leadershipcoaching sessions!
.
.
#outdooradventures #sandiego #executivecoach #executivecoaching #leadershipdevelopment #leaderskipskills #outdooractivities #leadershipstrategies

36w

14 likes
SEPTEMBER 11, 2020

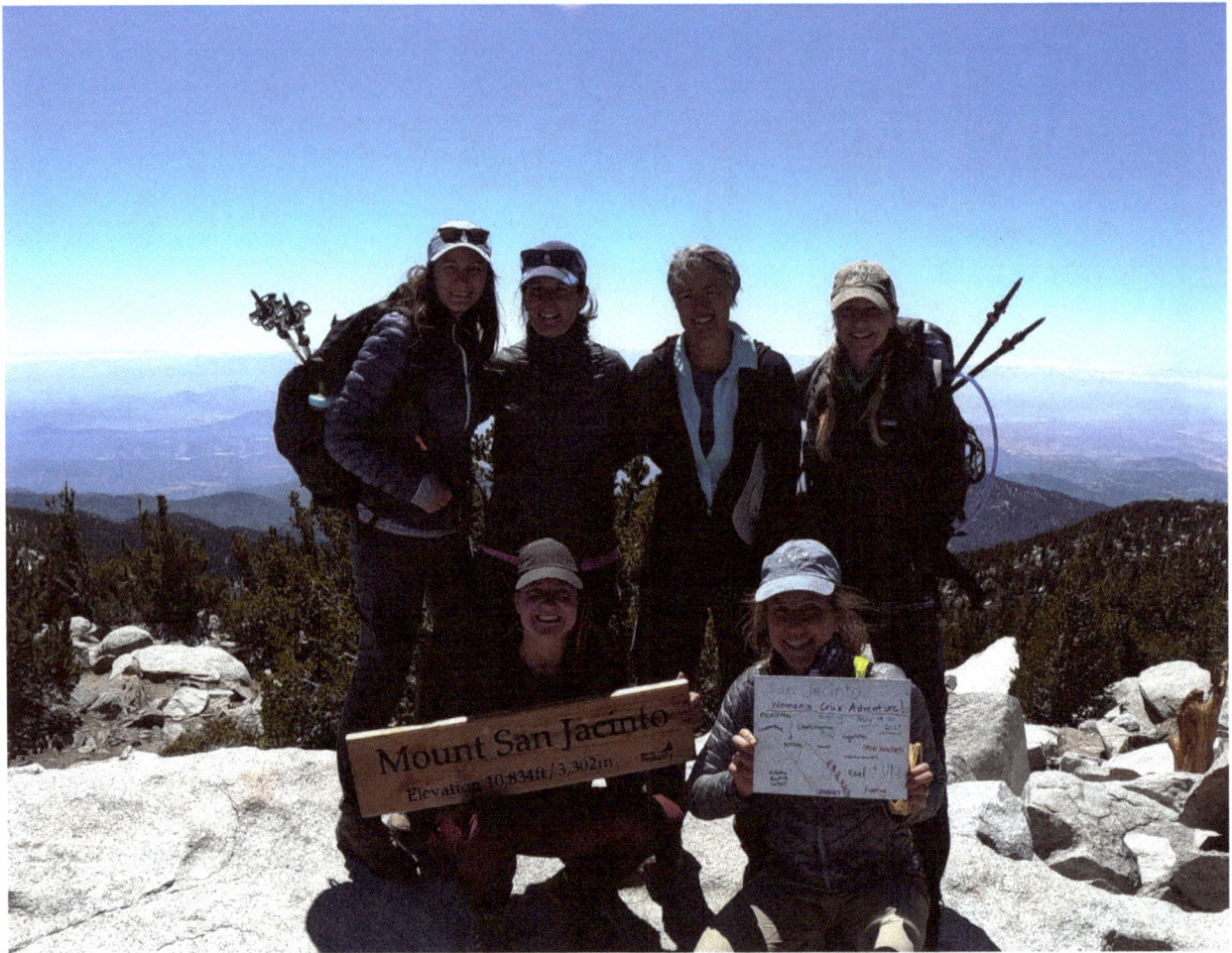

Website: www.cairnleadership.com

Instagram: @cairnleadership

Trademark and images used with permission.

Explorer Example #3: Exclusive Sicily Tours with Connie Costa
—Connie Costa, Founder

Connie Costa's Tours exemplify not only the Soulfluent® Explorer's love of travel but also a key way through which they learn and grow. Her exclusive and meticulously crafted tours of her beloved Sicily offer a high-touch travel experience that invites you to delight in your senses through food and to connect with your inner love of life while meeting other like-minded adventurers and foodies. In the process, you discover new or even long-dormant parts of your soul that are invigorated through the most decadent travel adventure customized to your every desire and whim.

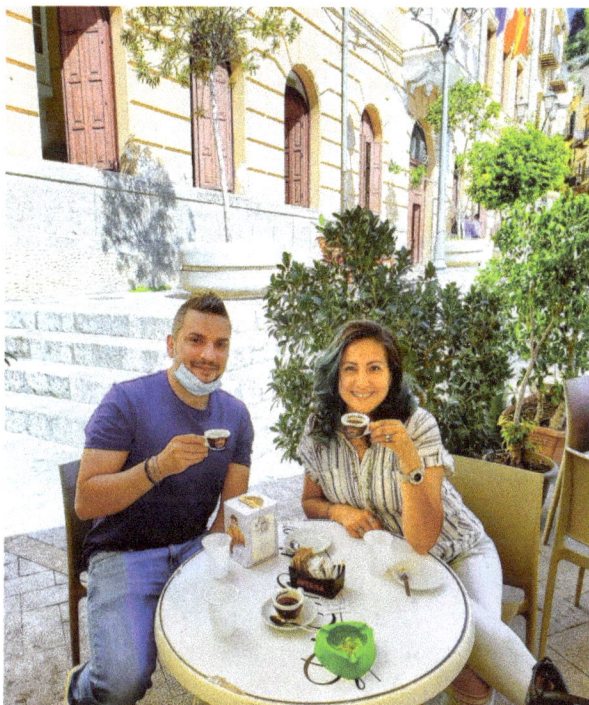

exclusivesicilytours
Sicily, Italy

exclusivesicilytours My beloved cousin @daniele84pa and I are ready for the tourists! We will welcome you with open arms. 😊😊😊😊😊
#sicily
#italy
ExclusiveSicilyTours.com
.
.
.
.
.
.
.
.

#instatravel #livetravelchannel
#traveldiaries #travelling
#travelphotography #traveladdict

37 likes
3 DAYS AGO

exclusivesicilytours
Saline di Trapani

· · ·

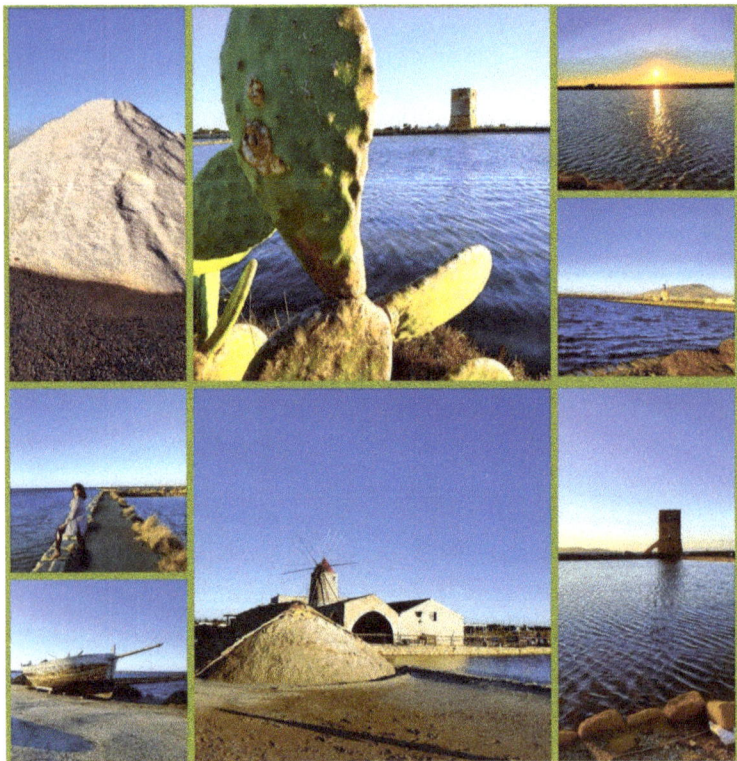

exclusivesicilytours Saline di Trapani
in #sicily #italy
Join me ▤❤🧡💛
ExclusiveSicilyTours.com

·
·
·
·
·
·
·

·

#instatraveling #traveldeeper #traveller
#worldtraveler #travelers #travelgram
#igtravel #traveling #travelling
#travelgirl #travelphoto #travelblogger
#travelpics #travellife #travel #travels
#mytravelgram #travelawesome
#traveler #traveldiaries #instatravel

♡ ◯ ◁   ▢

21 likes
NOVEMBER 13, 2020

☺ Add a comment...

exclusivesicilytours
Mondello, Sicilia, Italy

exclusivesicilytours "To have seen Italy without having seen Sicily is not to have seen Italy at all, for Sicily is the clue to everything!" - Goethe
.
Join me in paradise.
#sicily
#italy
.
.

exclusivesicilytours
Sicily, Italy

exclusivesicilytours It cannoli get better!
#sicily
#italy
ExclusiveSicilyTours.com
.

.
.
.
.

#foodanddrinks #foodart #foodadventure #foodartblog #foodaddiction #foodartchefs #foodadventures #foodagram #food_instalove #foodamology #foodaddicts #food_of_our_world #foodandtravel #foodaffair
#foodaddicted #food4thought

25 likes
JANUARY 13

exclusivesicilytours
Palermo, Italy

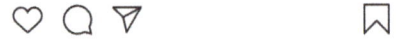

exclusivesicilytours Every single bar in #sicily has a story to tell.
😊 😊 😊 😊
#italy
ExclusiveSicilyTours.com
.
.
.
.
.

#foodblog #food #healthyfood #foodie #foodpic #foodpics #foodart #fooddiary #foodphotography #foodgram #foodies #foods #foodporn #foodlover #realfood #instafood #goodfood #fitfood #italianfood #foodgasm #lovefood #foodblogger #streetfood #foodstyling #foodlovers #foodstagram #travel #palermo

29 likes

NOVEMBER 6, 2020

Website: www.exclusivesicilytours.com

Instagram: @exclusivesicilytours

Trademark and images used with permission.

Soulfluent® Explorer Marketing

Content, Including Social Media

Your content is engaging, interactive, experiential, inspiring, rich in storytelling, and focuses equally on satisfying and uplifting the audience. Take your audience on an adventure with you. You are light, fun, and the life of the party, so share experiences and invite people to try them for themselves. Let people see you (create intimacy) and share what you care about (values and impact). Ask for support for causes you believe in, as you are a natural at enrollment and inspiring people.

Think rich, logical, inspiring, image-driven content. Describe processes when needed. When sharing your big ideas, make your content engaging and easy to follow. Showcase your out-of-the-box and innovative thinking with visually stimulating, people-oriented, emotionally driven concepts. Make sure the context for your message is clear.

Lead Generation

You attract people through people and through experiences. Give people a taste of an experience and then invite them to deeper and richer experiences with you as you highlight how they will transform.

It's best for Explorers to engage in person and out in the world. You'll want to have core systems and automation in place so you can be hands-off on the business side and focus on curating rich experiences.

You are great at sales conversations. Let your experiences speak for themselves, including the vision you are selling, and including the possibilities you are creating and the outcomes you can deliver.

Soulfluent® Explorer Business Model

You need a clear pipeline with offers that show people exactly where they are going next. Allow space for plenty of experiences and personal exploration that are not tied to a schedule. Focus on high-touch, high-outcome results that invite adventure, community, connection, and the ability to explore multiple things without always feeling the need to reach a specific outcome, rather understanding the power of the journey itself.

Keep it roomy. Don't feel like you need to focus on just one thing. You have different interests that may not appear connected, but they are connected by a greater mission, by your love of people, and by your willingness to try new things and do things differently.

Nothing about your business model is conventional, and yet it leans on tried and true methods that create focused results. Don't take too long to initiate, because you're always ready for the next project when it's time to move on. Your business model, offerings, and structure have a natural rhythm and cycle that puts you in sync with your own natural rhythms of creativity, travel, solo time, people time, etc.

As an Explorer you are quick out of the blocks. Make sure to get support and to keep track of the steps for implementing your idea so you don't have to play catch-up because you ignited the idea without enough forethought and planning.

Systems and Processes

You will thrive with highly automated operations and systems that use a small, close-knit team of people to handle the mundane administrative and day-to-day details of running the business. These elements will give you the freedom to be creative and to follow your own rhythm while having enough structure to move projects along and see them to fruition.

Ideal Clients

Your clients are diverse, multifaceted, and multicultural, with multiple interests. They have big visions, big hearts, and a big desire to make a big change in the world. They are curious and willing to do the deep inner work to create the lifestyle, dreams, and impact they desire.

They come from different lifestyles and backgrounds and appreciate the diversity of experiences that fascinates and inspires the Explorer (such as travel and inner work that allows them to discover new parts of themselves). Super-smart and motivated, they are curious about the world, life, and themselves. They love people and creating things on their own. It's a perfect match made in heaven.

Offer Types

Your offers are highly experiential, exploratory, exceptionally focused, and they require personal development work and action to implement. They are diverse, often shorter in duration (or offered only at specific times of the year), objective, and outcome-based through a proprietary and highly engaging process of personal exploration and inquisition. Look for ways to make them sustainable: series-based offers…longer outdoors adventures…masterminds…whatever feels right for you.

Soulfluent® Explorer
Team Building

Who You Need on Your Team

As an Explorer, you are highly appreciative and motivated, full of fun and exciting ideas that are innovative, creative, and inspiring to put into motion. You need someone who can handle a series of ongoing ideas thrown at them all at once, someone who is fabulous at taking over *all* of the details of your business/organization/life/operation so that you can focus on doing what you do best: networking, dreaming, exploring, traveling, talking to people, thinking up new ideas, inspiring people to dream and to actualize their dreams and to start creative projects.

Because you aren't afraid to fail, you're a quick starter and need team members who can help you with implementation, execution, team building, systems, and processes. You need simple, reliable, solid structures and loyal and reliable team members who know your personality and nuances well and can give you space to be creatively, geographically, and strategically free to do things on your own terms.

Your best team members:

- Are curious and multi-passionate, yet still grounded and focused on systems and structures.

- Love people and interfacing with customers and clients.

- Are pragmatic, fast, confident, detail-oriented.

3 things for *you* to remember:	3 things for *your team* to remember:
1. Include a few trusted people on your team who understand your big vision and are masterful technicians.	1. You move fast, so they should ask questions before diving in. Checklists are crucial!
2. Communicate your (high) expectations clearly, including timelines and details—and then let your team do the rest.	2. You can take your work too seriously. Your team can help you keep perspective and lessen worry so you can help them keep moving the job forward.
3. You will want to micromanage. Don't.	3. You must focus to complete a project, so they should provide clear deadlines for what they need from you.

If you are working with an Explorer

Know that you will always be stimulated; there will rarely be a dull moment. Stay on your toes. That being said, if the Explorer becomes overstimulated or overwhelmed, they will deflate emotionally and sink into depression, start doubting themselves, become reclusive, and lose their creative flow. Be mindful of the Explorer starting to slip to one extreme of their emotional spectrum and support them in finding an emotional balance point.

Invite them to infuse pleasurable activities and self-care back into their regimen, to surround themselves with people they love who can reflect back to them their magic and everything they love about life. Explorers aren't too easily affected by the world's expectations or fears, but it's important to know your *own* triggers and how to defuse them so you can bring yourself back to your vibrant, bubbly self. You need help in refining ideas—specifically, dialing in all the details for a full understanding of a project's ramifications and complexities, including financial costs and the personal involvement required (especially on a recurring basis). This way, you can be fully on board and completely aware of what you are stepping into.

Soulfluent® Explorer Mindset

Money Consciousness

Given your high-caliber skill set, you are innately gifted at making money, yet money isn't a prime motivation for you. Instead, you are motivated by ideas, adventure, flexibility, and freedom (your top value). The more you acknowledge your money desires and financial needs, the freer you will be to continue to achieve and/or expand your quality of life.

Visibility Consciousness

Explorers tend to be the life of the party. You love people, and you love to communicate about causes you trust. Your visibility edge centers around your innovative and at times out-of-the-box work, but with practice, selling can become a way for you to share something that matters deeply to your audience. This will be a process you enjoy.

You may feel confined, trapped, misunderstood, unappreciated, alone, overwhelmed, mistrustful of self and others.

Explorers are beloved because of the way they exude positivity, spark possibilities, and provide enthusiastic support for others who are going after their dreams. However, many people don't understand Explorers' highly adventurous free spirit and try to make sense of it by putting them in boxes that make them feel trapped and misunderstood. As a result, Explorers can struggle with feeling free to completely be themselves.

Tips:

- **Create a trusted inner circle.** These should be people that support your dreams, understand how you think, and are there to help you through adversity.
- **Have fun.** Spending time in nature, with animals, and having experiences that connect you to your adventurous spirit and that bring levity to your heart will recalibrate your perspective and provide the breath of crisp air you need to tackle your problem with fresh eyes.
- **Ask expansive questions.** Lean into your superpower of curiosity and start asking questions that will create new possibilities and expand your perspective.
- **Good is good enough.** You can always improve as you go but getting a project launched will provide more energy and momentum than perfectionism ever will.

When you want to reconnect to the energy of your Soulfluent® Explorer Archetype or need a boost to help you trust yourself and your way of doing things, come back to these phrases:

Where are we going next?

What's my next adventure?

Question everything.

What else is possible?

Let my imagination soar.

What my clients are saying....

Soulfluent® Explorer Archetype

"I see my "soul design" as an Explorer Archetype as a major asset.

Where society may have labeled my multifaceted interests as a negative, I've learned to embrace the gift that it is to be curious, adventurous and to love exploring the world, people and myself.

Courage is my biggest superpower.

I do things most people are too afraid to do. My imagination, creativity and ability to take fast action are my other superpowers.

Perhaps one of the greatest gifts of the Soulfluent® Leadership body of work is the PERMISSION it gives you to be yourself, just the way you are, without feeling the sense of obligation to be anything different to fit in or to appease others.

How liberating! This is the only way I want to live my life."

~Annie Sisson
Women's Empowerment Coach + Business Strategist

The Soulfluent® Explorer Leadership Archetype at a Glance

Dominant Motivation to Lead
Creating new possibilities.

Gifts
Imagination, inspiration, and connection. Passionate dreamers and adventurers, lovers of people and collaboration; travelers. Experiential leaders.

Challenges
Grounding vision and communication in practicality, diffuse awareness (needs structure to stay focused), hard to please.

Key Roles + Descriptors
Connector, Visionary, Teacher + Guide, Catalyst, Adventurer, Experiential Leader.

Message	Marketing
Dream, explore, and go for it. There's no time like the present, so live your dreams Go on your grandest adventure. Live out your mission and you make a difference. Enjoy your life to the fullest; don't hold back. Do it your way.	Interactive, engaging, experiential storytelling. Out of the box, show and tell that enrolls and invites. Dreamy, contemplative, thought-provoking. Resonant, intimate, deep, insightful, truth-telling, personal.

Vision, Impact, + Money

A world that works for everyone, where people can follow dreams and don't wait to go after what they want. Perfection, wholeness, interconnectedness, freedom, possibilities.

Money Consciousness: Trust that money is there to support your adventures and your dreams once you get into the right relationship with it. Use it and leverage it for your personal advantage and for the betterment of the world and the causes you believe in.

Business Model + Offer Types

Business Model: Scalable (if desired), personal, high-touch, allows for deep transformation, in-person offerings and virtual; travel. Unapologetic about how it makes the client uncover new parts of themselves and to go after what they want. Exploration is better when it creates something you haven't tried before.

Offer Types: Highly experiential offers that are super-focused, exploratory, and invite personal work as well as action to implement. Diverse, often shorter duration (or offered only at specific times of the year), objective- and outcome-based through a proprietary and highly engaging process of personal exploration and inquisition.

Explorer Mantra:

What's my next adventure?

The Soulfluent® Explorer Reflection Questions

1. What do you enjoy most about being an Explorer?

2. How do you navigate living in a world that aspires to live like you but doesn't often do it?

3. What do you love most about inspiring people to be adventurous?

4. How does travel expand your view of the world?

5. How do you navigate having multiple interests and staying focused?

6. What does freedom mean to you, and how does it inform your life and business decisions?

7. Where has your sense of adventure taken you?

8. How do you manage when people don't seem to get you or judge you or try to fit you into a box?

9. How has being an Explorer positively influenced how you run your business?

The Soulfluent® Divine Feminine Leadership Archetype

"I lead through creating community. Together we rise."

Overview of the Soulfluent® Divine Feminine Leader

The Divine Feminine Leader is a lover of life, people, beauty, nature, community, and the world. You love creating new possibilities through your individual contribution and through strategic collaborations that are designed to support a mission and vision greater than yourself. You are always seeking ways to create a win-win and not leave anyone behind.

You believe all people are equals and deserve equal access to opportunities and experiences. You may be highly welcoming, making your inclusive position known in all of your marketing. You live life according to your own rules (which makes some jealous; they wish they had the same courage). You function according to your own flow and rhythm. You are also incredibly smart and multitalented, which means you've excelled at a variety of jobs, businesses, and tasks. On paper, your career trajectory may not seem logical, but upon further inspection it's clear that each step on your journey has showcased one of your innate gifts at simplifying processes and concepts in innovative ways. You are a breath of fresh air in places where things were always done "old school," making room for people to connect, trust themselves, and trust your intuition. You nourish yourself through major self-care, taking time off, being in nature, savoring good food, traveling, and spending time with people you love the most.

Dominant Motivation to Lead:
Global community working together for the betterment of all through love, joy, and collaboration.

Gifts:
Collaboration, mastery, and community-building.

Challenges:
Temperamental nature, accepting support from others, and practicing sufficient self-care.

The Soulfluent® Divine Feminine's Vision:

Your vision for the world is one where every one of your actions is informed by love (including self-love) and a harmonious community.

It's natural for you to ask things like:

"What would love do in this situation?"

"What would self-love choose?"

"How can I do this with and for my community?"

"How can we truly all rise together?"

The Divine Feminine is an endless invitation for us to see ourselves as a part of a greater, interconnected web of humans. When we live through this lens, we get to think more expansively about the impact we have on each other's lives and on the planet. In so doing, we expand our ability to receive and we also actively explore ways that we can positively impact others through our thoughts, actions, ideas, and human connection.

Soulfluent® Divine Feminine Manifestation Style:

You can literally, and often do, manifest in your sleep. You are so deeply connected to your own flow and the energies of the Universe that you can co-create very easily and seamlessly once you trust your process, your desires, and yourself to fully receive what you want to manifest.

Given your natural leadership style and design, manifesting likely comes easily to you. The key to manifesting is to stay open to fully receiving what you've asked for, without compromising the integrity of the desire or standing in the way of having the exact experience you want. You have a highly attuned sixth sense that perceives invisible energies and realms that provide Divine inspiration, guidance, synchronistic events, and people who can move your vision forward. All of this can, and often does, flow with ease—when you let it.

Don't overburden your calendar or your mind with other people's agendas. If you're new to manifestation, start out with smaller things and then build up to pursuing greater goals and desires. Above all, make sure you are having fun, staying nourished, playing, sharing the magic with friends, going out into nature, and celebrating yourself and what you are creating.

It's not uncommon for people to be openly or secretly jealous of your manifesting power. This can make you uncomfortable. But having fun manifesting is one of the best parts of life, right? And while some may be jealous of your powers, you excel at holding space for them to have as much ease manifesting as you do. Quite simply, you are an example of what's possible; you show that there is plenty of everything for everyone—if we only give ourselves permission to ask for it, choose it, and fully receive it.

Divine Feminine Manifestation Process:

- Allow things to flow. This is the key to opening all the portals of manifestation and fully welcoming your desires. Trust the process.

- Clear your physical energy daily. Each week, clear energy in your home, office, car, and any environments where you work.

- Pay attention to the energy of the company you keep. Stay clear of "Debbie downers." These can be people who are jealous of your success, who make you doubt your vision or the size of your ambition or who are comfortable just "getting by." You can still wish them well, but don't include them within your inner circle.

- Give yourself permission to fully articulate and envision your desire in the exact form that you want it. Trust your *full* vision.

- Practice exceptional self-care to keep yourself energized and in a high frequency as much as possible. This enables your receiving channels to operate at full capacity.

- Calibrate your chakras weekly if possible, and certainly monthly.

- Surround yourself with a supportive community of like-minded manifestors who hold space for your creations and fully witness, acknowledge, embrace, and celebrate you (this is key!).

- Have fun.

- Trust those you know will hold space for the vision you truly want.

- Snap your fingers and let the magic unfold.

Soulfluent® Divine Feminine Branding

Brand Message

"Together we rise, and we are all stronger as a result."

Brand Words

As you browse through the following branding words, keep in mind that it would be impossible to use all of them in your messaging and copywriting. Circle the words that you feel the most resonance with, and use these as your gauge for everything you create in your business.

Brand Words

love	self-love	alchemy	transformation	collective	community	community-building	Truth	wisdom	guide
mastery	self-mastery	connection	in-person	events	communal	all-together	inclusive	collaborative	equality
equity	non-hierarchical	accessible	caring	co-creation	gathering	fun	energizing	generative	shape-shifting
expansive	empowered	empowering	resourceful	resilient	receiving	activist	activism	feminist	feminism
heard	seen	held	healer	catalyst	champion of others	celebrate	celebration	connector	connections
networker	supportive	once-in-a-lifetime	magical	alchemical	artist	creator	beautician	magic-maker	nature
Mother Earth	Divine Feminine	leadership	leader	exploration	possibilities	self-care	nurturing	soulful	embodiment
nourishing	life-giving	life-affirming	intuitive	intuition	spiritual	energy	trust	self-trust	good food
chocolate	wine	greens	flow	in the flow	natural rhythm	cycles	seasons	elements	adventure
fluid	flexible	non-binary	routines	masculine	Divine Masculine	allowing	pushing	hardship	ease
ease-filled	greater purpose	greater good	something bigger/greater than myself	patriarchy	balance	sixth sense	deeper knowing	oracle	Divine timing
Divine energy	in alignment	in tune with	attunement	atonement	forgiveness	self-forgiveness	compassion	personal mastery	creativity
beauty	inspiration	inspired/inspiring	innovative	innovation	trailblazer	adventurer	forward thinker/thinking	new	fresh
ideas	soft	feminine	strong	possibilities	imagination	wonder	awe	rising	upheaval
uprising	next and new level	leaders	new paradigm	systems	processes	people	humane	humanity	creatrix
visionary	provocative	instigative	daring	unapologetic	inspiring	captivating	holistic	"done with you"	community-ed
abundance	plenty for everyone	binary	chakras	positive change	results	resonant	timely	authentic	daring

Brand Colors and Visuals

Rich colors that are inviting, welcoming, and even a little mysterious. Multi-colored, gold, metallics, warm colors, or jewel tones.

Clean, bold, crisp fonts with a hint of feminine touches such as scripts and symbols. Images are potent tools to create connection and resonance with the audience. If you create art, consider using your own images in your branding and marketing.

MAGENTA	INDIGO	PERSIAN BLUE	CRIMSON	GOLD	ROYALTY

Examples of Soulfluent® Divine Feminine Businesses

Divine Feminine Example #1: Maya Moon Co.
—Kathryn Rogers, Founder

Kathryn Rogers, Founder of Maya Moon Co., channeled her love of sustainably-sourced food, healing and community engagement to create Maya Moon Co—a company that sources cacao for a healthier world by offering decadent chocolate truffles, drinking chocolate, and chakra-specific meditations. From the start, Kathryn has invited her community to support her mission. It began with her crowdfunding campaign that raised over $25,000 to kickstart the company and then with her community-centric marketing efforts, where she invites people to gather for meditations, sound baths, and tasting events accompanied by her chocolate truffles. Her products are a delicious means to not only bring people together but also a catalyst to further conversations around what it means to sustainably source food, since every product directly supports small farmers in Peru and Ecuador as well as local beekeepers. Maya Moon invites us to heal ourselves through conscious choices, local and global connections, and activism.

MAYA | MOON

JOIN MOON CLUB

Limited Edition Truffles delivered to your door each month,
plus New Moon & Full Moon meditations.

START YOUR HEART-OPENING JOURNEY TODAY

DECADENT AND NOURISHING CHOCOLATE TRUFFLES & CEREMONIAL DRINKING CACAO TO ALIGN YOUR
ENERGY AND HARMONIZE ECOSYSTEMS WORLDWIDE

HEALTHY INDULGENCE

Decadent chocolate truffles made with organic ingredients, sweetened with raw honey and zero preservatives.

INGREDIENTS MATTER

Made with direct trade cacao from farmers collectives in Peru and Ecuador and raw honey from local beekeepers.

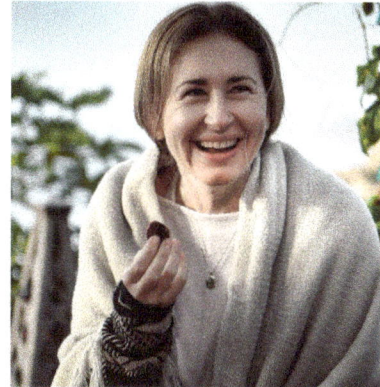

CACAO MEDITATIONS

Enjoy meditations with each delicious and distinctive flavor to elevate your energy and balance your body, mind and spirit.

mayamoonco • Following
Thegfbakingco

mayamoonco Thank you to everyone who joined us today at our first ever Pop Up Cacao Café! We loved seeing your smiling faces and sharing our artisan drinking cacao and truffles sourced with love from Ecuador and Peru.

Extra special thanks to @thegfbakingco for supporting small businesses and making this event possible. And thanks to @chocolatesanjose @mikolichhoney and @kajkabchocolate for the lovingly grown/gathered ingredients and @thelovecreatrix for sharing our cacao with so much joy❤️

Stay tuned for our February pop up café date to be announced soon!

mayamoonco • Following

mayamoonco ❤️ Start your heart-opening journey this year with our new monthly Moon Club subscription!

When you join our monthly Moon Club membership you'll receive:

1) A gift box of our limited edition, seasonal cacao truffles delivered to your door each month (4 pieces)
2) Monthly astrology forecast via email on the first of the month
3) Links to join our live and recorded New Moon and Full Moon meditations

A wonderful way to support your own heart-opening journey each month! Your membership supports organic farmers collectives in Peru and local, sustainable beekeepers.

36 likes

JANUARY 7

Add a comment...   Post

Website: www.mayamoon.co

Instagram: @mayamoonco

Trademark and images used with permission.

Divine Feminine Example #2: Hera Hub
—Felena Hanson, Founder

Hera Hub, an international female-focused co-working space and business accelerator for women entrepreneurs, based in San Diego, CA, exemplifies the Soulfluent® Divine Feminine Archetype qualities of community-building, inclusivity, and collaboration. Their business model supports members through education, mentoring, and collaboration while their spa-like co-working spaces give members access to a professional, productive space to grow a prosperous business built on the foundation of a powerful community. Through a series of in-person and online events ranging from networking mixers, workshops, business growth programs, and additional resources such as their podcast, they support women to be their best while spotlighting members, highlighting social issues, and inspiring women globally to thrive in business through community with a dash of fun and zen.

Flourishing Entrepreneurial Ecosystem

One of our members described Hera Hub as a "flourishing entrepreneurial ecosystem — a village pulsing with talent and heart." This description paints an accurate picture of our community.

The Hera Hub community is comprised of hundreds of female entrepreneurs who support one another through collaboration, resources, referrals, feedback and mentoring. From our platform, new businesses have been spurred, funding secured and life-long friendships built.

You are sure to find women in similar and related business situations that can assist you with the growth of your business. We serve women at all stages of business, in a variety of industries, including:

Technology | Finance | Marketing | Legal | Personal services | Education | Non-profit.

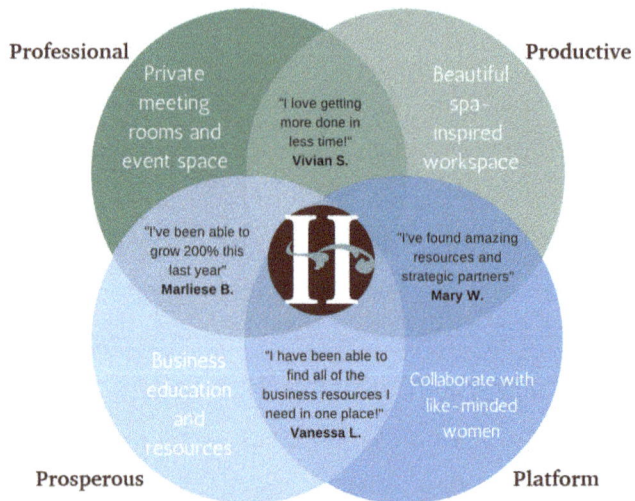

Professional · Productive · Prosperous · Platform

- Private meeting rooms and event space
- "I love getting more done in less time!" Vivian S.
- Beautiful spa-inspired workspace
- "I've been able to grow 200% this last year" Marliese B.
- "I've found amazing resources and strategic partners" Mary W.
- Business education and resources
- "I have been able to find all of the business resources I need in one place!" Vanessa L.
- Collaborate with like-minded women

herahub
Hera Hub

herahub Need a business reboot? Work one-on-one with Hera Hub's founder, @felenahanson, to re-engineer your path forward and make 2021 your best year yet.
You will walk away with a strategic road-map for the next 12 months... to help you pivot, think bigger, and identify the resources you need to make your goals a reality.
Link to learn more - https://www.facebook.com/events/4062941837103157

10w

queenmabmusic Go Felena!!!! 🔥🔥🔥

10w   2 likes   Reply

Liked by andreasilver_ and 93 others

APRIL 23

Add a comment...

herahub
Hera Hub

herahub Hera Hub implements CDC-compliant protocol to keep members and guests safe:

Signs have been placed throughout the space focused on cleaning and safety protocols.
A limited number of people will be allowed in the workspace at one time.

Practice physical distancing.
Wear masks when moving throughout the space.

For more information, email: info@herahub.com

18w

♡ ◯ ▽   🔖

Liked by **felenahanson** and **30 others**

FEBRUARY 19

Hera Hub Mission

To provide entrepreneurial women with a productive, professional work and meeting space, where they can connect with a like-minded community to collaborate and flourish.

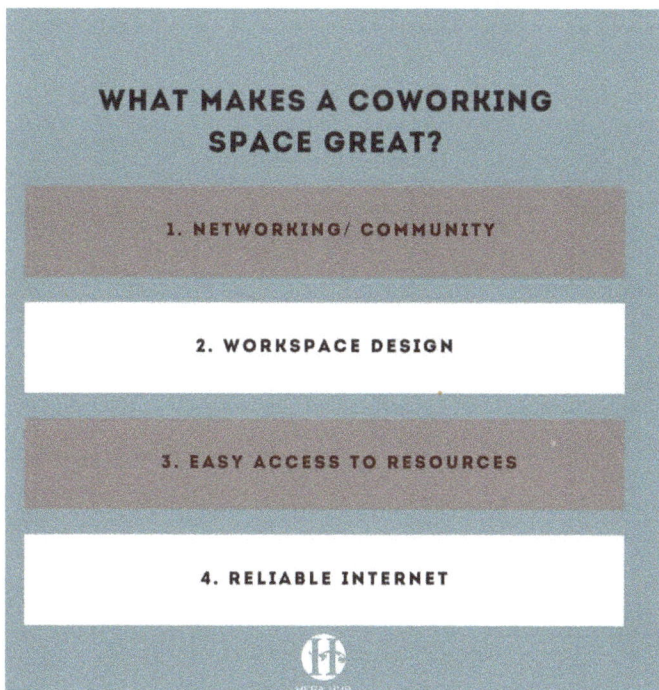

WHAT MAKES A COWORKING SPACE GREAT?

1. NETWORKING/ COMMUNITY

2. WORKSPACE DESIGN

3. EASY ACCESS TO RESOURCES

4. RELIABLE INTERNET

herahub
Hera Hub

herahub We want to know - what makes a coworking space great? Comment bellow!

#coworklocal #coworkingspaces #herahub

28w

westcoastdomer #1 - Having my own Hera Squad!!

28w 2 likes Reply

—— View replies (1)

felenahanson Community 🙌

28w 1 like Reply

♡ ◯ ▽   🔖

Liked by **katherinezacharias** and **23 others**

DECEMBER 16, 2020

☺ Add a comment...

Hera Hub Reminder

Sub-Hubs: Affinity groups within our Community. They are global, member-led groups that meet regularly to share resources and support one another.

Love It

Okay

❤ 1M

herahub
Hera Hub Mission Valley

herahub ✨MEMBERS ONLY✨

Have you heard about ours Sub-Hubs? Sub-Hubs are global, member-led, affinity groups, which meet regularly to share resources and support one another. Some Sub-Hubs are industry-specific, others have risen from common interests or goals, while others are based on the phase of business shared by the members. Each Sub-Hub has a private Facebook group for the sharing of resources, discussion, and events. The members of each group decide upon the format and structure of the virtual meetings. New members are always welcome, as are suggestions for new Sub-Hubs.

Liked by **corporatetocanvas** and 21 others
JUNE 17

ONE SMALL POSITIVE THOUGHT CAN CHANGE YOUR WHOLE DAY

herahub
Hera Hub

herahub Our thoughts are powerful. Be intentional with them and notice the shift in perception.

#stressawarenessmonth #positivethoughts #womeninbusiness #womenbusinessowners

12w

5_ringsfitness Yesss to this 🙌
12w 1 like Reply
—— View replies (1)

herahubcarlsbad 💯

Liked by **felenahanson** and 32 others
APRIL 5

Add a comment…   Post

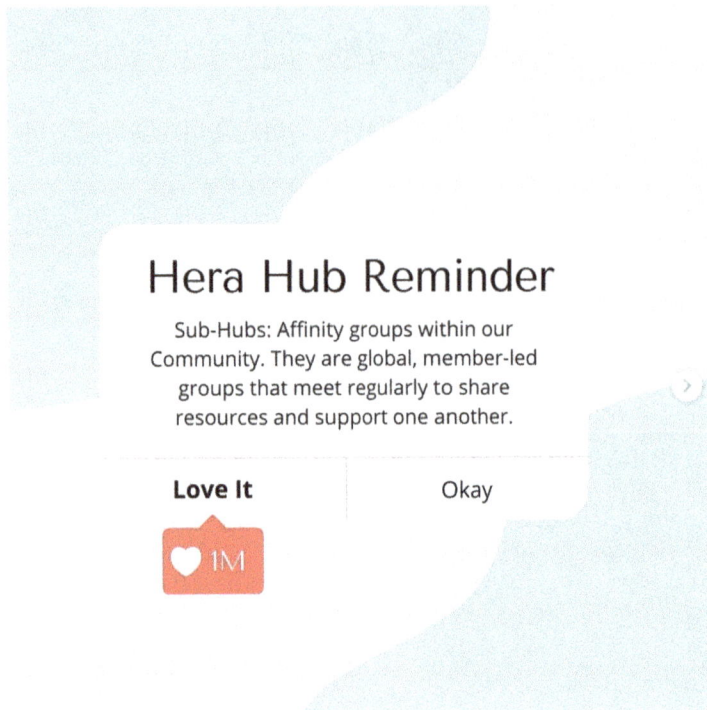

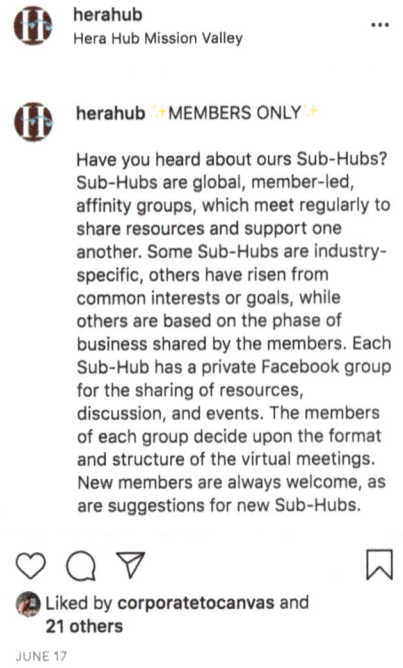

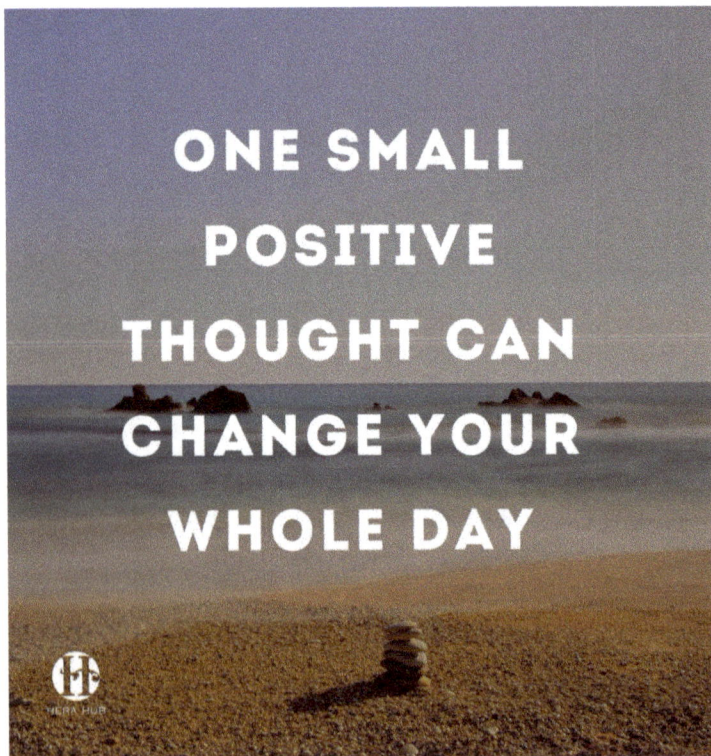

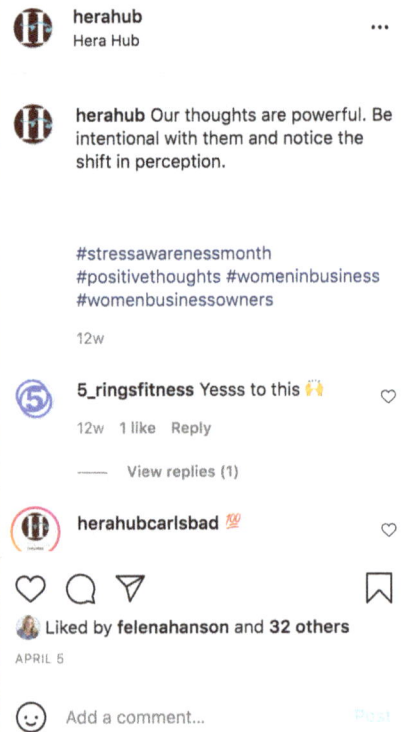

Website: www.herahub.com

Instagram: @herahub

Trademark and images shared with permission.

Divine Feminine Example #3: South LA Cafe
—Celia Ward-Wallace + Joe Wallace, Founders

South LA Cafe's motto of *Coffee. Connection. Community.* is the perfect encapsulation of the Soulfluent® Divine Feminine Archetype's superpower: being a catalyst for change through community-driven engagement. When COVID hit shortly after the South LA Cafe opened in the fall of 2019, co-founders Celia and Joe pivoted and began serving $35 sponsored bags of fresh food to local community members affected by the pandemic. Celia and Joe are proactive in inviting local community members to connect with others at their cafe—moreover, they are vocal in their call for social justice and economic equality through their marketing, speaking, and social media content. Bottom line: Celia and Joe are potent advocates for the betterment of their community and an inspiration to all who seek to do good for their communities through positive business practices. In their own words: "We are a black-led movement to provide racial, social, economic and food equity through our community business model."

southlacafe ✓ • Following
South La Cafe

southlacafe ✓ Hey y'all, folks are hungry, can you help us feed them? Every Wednesday we provide free and fresh groceries to over 200 families in need. We've done this for the past 30 weeks!!! But we need your help to keep it going. Each family can receive enough food for a family of four for only $35! Can you sponsor a local families groceries for this week? Yes? Here's what you need to know...

1. Click the link in our bio
2. Select "sponsor" a box
3. Select "milk" type
4. Select "bread" type
5. Select "store pickup"
6. Checkout and that's it! We'll distribute it tomorrow to a

Liked by **istandforlove** and **198 others**

JANUARY 12

Add a comment...

WHAT WE DO

We're on a mission to fight racial, social, economic, and food inequity through coffee, community, and connection.

WE PROVIDE HEALTHY & AFFORDABLE OPTIONS

Coffee, tea, soups, salads, sandwiches & fresh groceries!

We are committed to creating equal access to fresh and healthy options for our South LA community that can be found in other neighborhoods, but with pricing that is affordable.

WE ARE A SOUTH CENTRAL LA CULTURAL HUB

Book readings, workshops, art, music & activism!

We are committed to playing our part in keeping alive the vibrant culture and history of South Central Los Angeles. The SLAC will become your special spot in the neighborhood where you are always welcome!

"We started the South LA Cafe because, after decades of living in a food desert, we wanted fresh, affordable and healthy food options for ourselves and our neighbors. Instead of waiting for it to arrive, we decided to take a leap of faith and provide it ourselves."

-Celia & Joe Ward-Wallace, South LA Cafe

#INTHEGOODFOODZONE

southlacafe ✓
South La Cafe

today we celebrate Joe, the hardest working man in the neighborhood, for his heart and dedication to provide ACCESS to fresh, healthy, and affordable food to our South Central LA community! What started with a dream by one is now supported by the many! Together we are a Black-led movement to provide racial, social, economic, and food equity!
.
Your support of our café allows us to create a sustainable Community Business Model and provide jobs to local folks, create safe spaces, preserve and create culture, and open new cafés. Your sponsorship of groceries allows us to level the playing field, and provide free and fresh food to the community. Without your support, none of this work would be possible.

1,476 views
3 DAYS AGO

Website: www.southlacafe.com

Instagram: @southlacafe

Trademark and images used with permission.

Soulfluent® Divine Feminine Marketing

Content, Including Social Media

Your content is inspiring, engaging, interactive, and inviting. It's concise, emotion-evoking, and truth-telling, and it invites people into a new possibility. It's positive, real, and focused on storytelling. Include experiential, dynamic, animated (such as drawings or video), and behind-the-scenes content that guides, shows, and illuminates the new way forward.

Lead Generation

Focus on a combination of virtual, automated, and people-driven leads with collaborations and strategic partnerships. Look at non-traditional options that are simple, effective, and sustainable—particularly those that pool resources so you aren't doing everything yourself.

Focus on collaborations and strategic partnerships. Since community is your focus, look for people in your community with whom you can collaborate. It's important that the people you collaborate with are also focused on benefiting the greater good rather than what they can get from you and your community.

Consider lead-generation methods that are out of the box. When everyone is doing things in a certain way, look for energy that will benefit the community as a whole and ask yourself how you can do it differently. Focus on simple and sustainable methods; self-care is essential as you grow your business and communities.

Soulfluent® Divine Feminine Business Model

Scalable, spacious, focused, primarily group- and community-oriented, with some room for smaller or 1:1 projects. Divine Feminine businesses are best designed for groups and in some cases the masses, so focus on creating spacious and scalable containers (long-term group programs, membership sites, community-driven projects) and strategic partnerships where you don't have to do everything yourself. Certification models can also be a good fit, as they focus on community and on reaching the public with your body of work in broader, often community-based, ways.

Systems and Processes

Automation, automation, automation.

It is essential to implement simple, clear, and sustainable processes, systems, and automated sequences for every key aspect of the business. Cultivate a tight team that handles the day-to-day and the details of running the business/project so you have space to nourish your energy and creativity. These systems will help keep your mood high, your spirit inspired, and your imagination active so you truly enjoy what you are creating as it is being built.

You love flow. Once you understand that simple structures actually support and enhance your flow, the more you will be willing and able to incorporate flow into your life and business.

Ideal Clients

Your ideal clients are intuitive, sensitive, smart, highly ambitious, generative, and driven to contribute. They love people and are highly skilled at what they do. They are ready to be in community and to scale and grow vis-à-vis their outer projects and personal development. Your ideal clients are open to exploratory, engaging, and thought-provoking conversations that lead to magical thinking, projects, and innovation that wouldn't have otherwise been created.

Offer Types

Create offers that are community based and collaborative, focusing on groups and shorter-term individual offers (1:1 work). Your most effective offers are deep, journey-driven, community/group-based, and focused on the fact that everyone is in it together: "Together we rise."

Soulfluent® Divine Feminine Team Building:

Who You Need on Your Team

Divine Feminine leaders are incredible at creating community and can see the gifts in others. However, you don't always trust those who are close to you, and often you don't feel confident that you can effectively lead your team. At times, you can let old wounds get in the way of trusting yourself to be a good team leader and team builder. As you build your team, you must be extra clear with yourself as to what you desire, establish very clear expectations, and give people the benefit of the doubt. Learn to trust your instincts when you see a red flag during hiring or with an existing team member. Be willing to speak up firmly and kindly, and move forward. Don't keep team members involved because you feel bad about letting them go, avoid uncomfortable conversations, or are unwilling to see where you need to improve your communication skills and expectations.

Tight, efficient, virtual teams that work in their zones of genius and can work independently and as a part of a team are good for you. You are here to empower your team to be their best and to create in community and through collaboration while giving you space to work independently. A project manager can guide the pacing of your projects, keep you in check, and manage other team members. You'd much rather map out the plan, share it with your project manager, and then have them interface with the rest of the team.

Communication is your greatest edge and can be your greatest source of discord. Be vigilant about sharing exactly how you want something to be executed. Give people trial runs (30 or 90 days) before you fully entrust them with the intimate details of your intellectual property, creativity, innermost thoughts, and inner circle of contacts.

One of your greatest leadership edges lies in your willingness to trust that your team can not only embrace your vision but also earn your trust. When you are willing to ask for and fully receive support, you will be golden—and as the huge burden leaves your shoulders, it will be replaced by a massive SURGE of creativity and spaciousness. This is what you've been craving all along.

Your best team members:

- Are loyal, communicative, and dependable; they do what they say they will do.

- Love being a part of a team and mission that's greater than themselves. They contribute ideas and aren't afraid to make mistakes and to try new things.

- Communicate clearly and honor boundaries to do their best work. They work hard and play hard.

3 things for *you* to remember:

1. Awesome team members exist and are trustworthy. They will make your life so much easier and joyful—and they have a lot to teach you as well.

2. Clarify instructions and then ask your team to clarify what they think you said. Make all expectations exceptionally clear.

3. Finding a team's flow takes time and is worth the effort. Trust your gut in your hiring process. Hire for trial runs—and fire promptly, when you know it's time.

3 things for *your team* to remember:

1. Be on the same page. Learn the team motto and get clear on the vision, values, and mission of the operation.

2. Be patient as the Divine Feminine leader learns to trust you.

3. Encourage the Divine Feminine leader to practice self-care and boundary-setting—and then emulate these for yourself.

If you are working with a Divine Feminine

Know that while they genuinely want things to work out, they may not yet fully trust themselves as leaders and may hold their "secrets" close to the chest. They may have high expectations and tend toward becoming distant, cold, rigid, and unsympathetic when things aren't delivered in the way they imagined. Key strategies for optimizing results include:

- understanding their expectations and timelines
- asking them to share their full vision with you
- being willing to manage the project from start to end
- being willing to refine and/or reconstruct their systems and processes (in collaboration and in co-creation with them).

Divine Feminine leaders dream of being able to hand over all the administrative, technology, and day-to-day tasks of their business to you, yet it also terrifies them. For this reason, it is critically important to go gently and to avoid coming in and trying to run the show before you have buy-in. Even if the Divine Feminine leader says they are ready, it's wise to double-check with them and to intuitively read between the lines and notice the degree of warmth or coldness in their tone and communications.

While genuine and warm, Divine Feminine leaders have a deliberate and cooler side to them when they are focused on the big picture or when they are afraid, hurt, or when boundaries have been overstepped. It's important to be patient with them, to be willing to apologize and to make things right, and to be honest every step of the way about what you are capable of—both regarding your actual skill set as well as the timeframe of operation and creation. Since the Divine Feminine leader is so focused on the big vision that impacts many people, they can come across as short and to-the-point. It's important to not take this personally.

Divine Feminine leaders are pretty committed to taking time off on the weekend and making space for self-care; it would behoove their team members to prioritize self-care practices as well. You don't have to be on the same schedule, but you know the value of taking time off to be creative, spend quality time with family, and generally unplug from work.

Divine Feminine leaders have strong, often hard-earned boundaries. If these boundaries are overstepped and/or loyalty or value is broken, it may be hard to regain their trust. At the very least, expect a cooling period as the trust is repaired.

Soulfluent® Divine Feminine Mindset

Money Consciousness

While you don't often start off with a great relationship to money, you do have an innate ability to manifest money, resources, opportunities, and synchronistic events that help you to create what you desire. Once you heal your relationship to money and realize that you have always had the ability use it to create magic, you can trust yourself more to create, keep, and multiply your wealth. You will also build confidence in your potency to create and retain money despite any judgments from others.

Divine Feminine Leaders are designed to be champion creators and multipliers of money, hence your innate ability to "manifest" it as if on demand or by magic. Trusting your power to create money and to be a good steward of it (and that there will be some people that won't appreciate you for it) is a part of your edge.

This may not be what you're currently experiencing with your money. If so, consider this a reminder of what's possible, what's innate within you. Aligning and integrating your Soulfluent® Divine Feminine Leadership Archetype is your next step toward creating this kind of flow with wealth in your life.

> Divine Feminine leaders are here to design, create, and multiply money in new paradigms, structures, and containers that invite equality, equity, sustainability, and a deliciously freeing fluidity.

Visibility Consciousness

While incredibly engaging and amazing connectors and lovers of people, Divine Feminine leaders don't always start off feeling comfortable "in front of the camera." The more you find and trust your ways of doing things, of connecting authentically in a "business" way and trust your innate ways of doing things (which will definitely not be in the norm—and often will be inspired) then you can relax, enjoy the show, and focus on the project at hand: having fun, staying light-hearted, and creating something bigger in community than you would have on your own.

When they attempt to take on the responsibilities of others, Divine Feminine leaders may feel unappreciated, temperamental, or overburdened and may become distrustful of others or feel taken advantage of. When they are out of alignment, they can feel anxious (shallow breathing), experience a need to control people or situations, take frantic action based on the desire to see movement rather than trusting the process, or have difficulty knowing things can get handled without their involvement.

Avoiding the Pitfalls

With their appealing and magnetic energy, zest for life, and love of people and connection, Divine Feminine leaders are a delight to be around. However, they can make mistakes or become resentful and unpleasant when they over-give, try to take on too much, fail to pace themselves, or neglect to give themselves the care they need. They can return to alignment by taking a walk or a bath, reading, spending time alone in nature or in silence, ensuring they get sufficient rest, nutrition, and hydration.

Tips:

- **Ask for help more often than you feel comfortable doing.** As good as you are at multitasking, doing everything alone quashes your mojo, dilutes your creativity, and slows your progress. All the more reason for having a trusted small team that has your back.

- **Strong boundaries are your friend.** It is important to prioritize your sanity and love of self over continually helping others with "just one more thing"— even when that comes easily to you. Consider putting gatekeepers in place so you don't have to constantly say no.

- **Structure creates more flow.** Structure actually allows you to be more spontaneous, because it provides clear parameters within which to create, lead, and live. It can be as simple as clearly defining and communicating your work hours and off hours, taking vacation days, compiling a list of tasks to delegate, implementing processes and systems that keep you from constantly reinventing the wheel.

- **Create a tight inner circle that knows you well and reminds you to rest and replenish.** Being a change-maker and fighting for the collective good can be exhausting. Make sure you spend time with friends who make you laugh, who remind you of what makes you so awesome, who lighten the weight in your heart and help you enjoy life. You also need friends with whom you can share your deepest thoughts and emotions—friends who are willing to go deep as you go.

- **Add in more white space on your calendar than you think you'll need.** Holding space for time that has no purpose creates room to connect with yourself, play, nourish your body, replenish your spirit, and to simply *be*.
- **Don't let your day run *you*.** To avoid this, follow a routine that supports you in feeling energized and grounded, nourished and well-hydrated.

Divine Feminine Mantras

When you want to reconnect to the energy of your Soulfluent® Divine Feminine Archetype or need a boost to help you trust yourself and your way of doing things, come back to these phrases:

I rest when needed.

I love to go with the flow.

I know when I'm out of my flow.

*Anything is possible when we collaborate and
do things together and for each other.*

No womxn left behind.

We are all in this together.

Soulfluent® Divine Feminine Archetype

"I think this is the first time I've actually thoroughly believed in what I was selling and in myself to deliver something really valuable not because the product is different but because the self-doubt isn't there anymore.

Having the messaging clearly reflect the truth of what my work offers in words that ring deeply true for me and how I deliver value is a big piece of that.

Having Priscilla hold my hand through the entire process of building my online Vibrant Presence Community membership went above and beyond what I expected and made the process faster and easier than I thought was possible. I have created an offering I'm proud of and that allows me to help more people and still have time to be with my family and to do what I love."

~Cassie Nevitt

Art of Feminine Presence™ licensed teacher

The Soulfluent® Divine Feminine Reflection Questions:

1. What is it about the Divine Feminine energy that feels so mysterious, energizing, and magnetic?

2. What does being in flow look and feel like for you?

3. When did you finally stop trying to do things the conventional way and start trusting in your own flow to live, love, and lead?

4. What do you love about your ability to create communities that support the greater good?

5. What self-care practices do you lean into to stay grounded, nourished, and energized?

6. How have you learned to keep yourself in flow? How do you navigate some of your challenges such as over-giving, trying to do everything yourself, and difficulty trusting others?

7. What is your advice for other Divine Feminine leaders, including possible pitfalls, as they seek to create their own generative communities?

The Soulfluent® Divine Feminine Archetype at a Glance

Dominant Motivation to Lead
To build community and collaboration; to increase love and connection.

Gifts
Collaboration, mastery, community-building.

Challenges
Temperamental, hesitancy to accept support from others, difficulty in practicing self-care.

Key Roles + Descriptors
Collaborator, Connector, Catalyst, Receiver, In the Flow.

Message	Marketing
Together we rise. We are stronger when we work together. Collaboration, community, stronger together. Beauty, nourishment, flow, feminine strengths and power are the future. Self-care is the way.	Heart-led, resonant, deeply caring and spiritual. Instigates new possibilities. Catalyst to make people stop and think. Genuine, inspired, and inspiring. Beauty-driven, creative, fluid and in flow. In sync with nature, the seasons, the cycles of life. Magical, fun, innovative, ease-filled, streamlined.

Vision, Impact, + Money

A world where everyone thrives through community, collaboration, and building new paradigms. A world that is visionary, provocative, instigative, daring, unapologetic, inspiring, holistic. We heal through interconnectedness and grow through togetherness.

Money Consciousness: Acknowledge your natural ability to create money, and give yourself permission to have it all, to have it your way, and to be right in your relationship with building wealth if so desired. Can build feminine empires that change worlds and can allow money to amplify, multiply, and work for the greater good.

Know the power of sacred commerce.

Business Model + Offer Types

Business Model: Scalable, community-driven and community-based—groups, collaborative, contribution-focused, personal, high-touch, allows for deep transformation, in-person offerings and travel, lots of time in beautiful places and spaces.

Offer Types: Community-focused and driven by the greater good; collaborative, groups. Shorter-term individual (1:1 work). Deep, journey-driven offers, focusing on the fact that everyone is in it together: "Together we rise."

Divine Feminine Mantra:

"No womxn left behind.
We are all in this together."

Conclusion

The time is upon us to show up and to create the world we know is possible if we each rise up and do our part.

As the world calls out for our leadership contribution, the path forward is to say yes to ourselves, to our vision of what's possible, and to do so within a new paradigm: One where everyone wins, not just a select, privileged few.

This book is a guide to support you in understanding your soul's leadership language and learning how to apply it to every core aspect of your life and business so you operate from a space of deep alignment, joy, and fulfillment.

Gone are the days that we sacrifice ourselves, our well-being, our self-expression, and our joy for the sake of success and money.

Now is the time to rise up, to normalize a future where every single human being matters, every voice counts, and every act of kindness and awareness has the potential to create a potent ripple effect of change across the planet.

Soufluent® Leadership is a framework that supports you in creating 360° wins: by this I mean that your conscious choices get to have a positive impact that radiates far beyond you. Your personal and business choices get to support not only you and your immediate circle, family, and community but also your team members, your town, your customers, the planet, and the collective good.

Soulfluent® Leadership is ultimately about creating win-win-wins that support and include all. Radical concept, right?

When you know yourself better, you lead better. At the very least, that knowledge creates greater self-awareness that supports you in making higher-level decisions that consider the greater good over tangential or impulsive decisions that come from egoic urges, agendas, or simply out of fear.

The antidote to fear is courage, and that is an easier pill to swallow when you are tuned into your essence: both you and your soul know how to use your knowledge of yourself (your "soul fluency") to make powerful change.

Archetypes, which have been around since the very beginning of time, provide a framework for understanding energies, patterns, and human nature that's normally housed in the collective unconscious. We've all heard about the Mother Archetype, the Warrior Archetype, the Goddess Archetype, and so on. While we may each have a unique mental image of what each Archetype might be, we still conjure up the same types of images, feelings, and perceptions because of that deeper familiarity.

> **The beauty of an Archetypal framework, and why we the soul guides and protectors of the Soulfluent® work shared it with me and hereby with you, is so you can tap into the potency of everything that's already within you.**

For too long, humans have been disconnected from their power because they've operated solely or primarily from their logical minds—not their inner knowing (i.e., their soul). Archetypes are a great way for us to tap into our inner knowing, our unconscious minds, and to bring all of our wisdom, magic, and gifts to the forefront and to operate from, make decisions from, and lead from a soul-aligned space that takes into account all of who we are.

Soulfluent® leaders are self-expressed, courageous, outspoken leaders with a unique vision for the betterment of the world.

We are no better or worse than anyone else and simply ask for the space within ourselves and in the world to bring our vision forth with grace, compassion, and groundedness.

What makes this work unique is that it invites you to tap into your energetic being (in other words, your soul) and to lead from a comprehensive, cohesive, and deeply aligned energy that's entirely YOU.

It's a reminder that you always have and always will have everything you need when you connect to your soul and lead from your innate strengths.

When you make choices and decisions from within yourself—as uncomfortable or scary as it may seem at times—you will always be stronger and better for it.

We don't say that it will always be easy...but it will be the most potent and ultimately the most gratifying choice for you—every time.

> **And while leading from your soul can be lonely, you don't have to do it alone. First, your soul and your soul guides, angels, and ethereal "team" are always ready, willing, and available to support you. You need only ask for guidance.**

Secondly, by holding this book in your hands, you are now a part of the Soulfluent® global family of leaders actively making the world a better place by leading from your soul and making your unique contribution from a conscious space of possibility, integrity, and authenticity.

Give yourself the time, energy, and space to integrate your primary Soulfluent® Leadership Archetype into your life and business. This work is rich, at times dense, and equally awe-inspiring if you give it a chance.

If you are willing to crack the surface, like the top of a crème brûlée, you may be surprised at the creamy goodness that awaits you below.

Savor this material.
Breathe life into it in your own timing.
Trust its wisdom, including your own.
Stay curious, in a state of inquiry.

> **Know that you don't need to have all the answers. You just need to stay connected to your soul's Truth and not waiver from its infinite wisdom.**

Don't discount the wisdom of your human body and its ability to guide you in making choices.

Soul decisions aren't made the same way as logical brain decisions.

They ask more of you. They ask you to trust more deeply. They ask you to look closer. Sometimes to leap without having any clue what the next step is or how to get to your next destination. They may ask you to make tough choices and to have uncomfortable conversations.

Do. It. Anyway.

You know you are up for the task.

You know that you are here for more.

Not because more is better, per se, but because more is possible and you want a better world for all and you are courageous enough to answer your call.

Yes—there will be tough moments.

There will be winding roads, detours, and ditches along the way. Expect it. It's not like it's unknown territory for you. You are strong and capable.

May your work integrating your Soulfluent® Leadership Archetype into your business be a joyful one.

Let it seep into your being like a delicious cup of warm tea.

Trust the process and let the magic reign supreme.

You've got this.

> **I believe in you and so does your soul—the deepest, truest part of you that will never leave you and that always has your back.**

To your sweet and soulful success.

−Priscilla

Take the Quiz
Discover Your Soulfluent® Leadership Archetype

Identifying your Soulfluent® Leadership Archetype will illuminate your innate leadership gifts, strengths, and leadership style, resulting in greater flow, ease, and fulfillment as you grow your business and share your vision for a better world for all.

Instructions:

Based on the energy from which you primarily operate, answer the following questions, honestly and with an open heart—not what you *wish* were true, but what actually is. And remember, each of the Archetypes have their own gifts and challenges.

You cannot get this quiz wrong, so don't let yourself start to overthink things. Just go with your first instinctive response and trust it.

The quiz contains nine questions and should take less than five minutes to complete.

Circle the letter to the left of your response that best applies to you.

Let's get started!

1. What do you think it takes to be a soulful leader?

   A. Guts and intuition
   B. The ability to think fast on your feet
   C. Taking the path less traveled
   D. Asking lots of questions and determining the consensus
   E. Gathering in community and co-creating the option that's the best for everyone

2. When you find yourself at a crossroads and don't know which way to turn, you tend to:

   A. Take a step back, pause, meditate, and see what feels like your next best aligned step to move forward
   B. Trust your inner knowing and take a bold move forward, no matter what the cost. The most important thing in this situation is to do the right thing for the greater good
   C. Pick an option that might be fun and exciting and give it a try
   D. Research the options online and then take a self-assessment to determine the best option
   E. Gather a group of people to brainstorm the options and see what's in everyone's best interest

3. When you decide it's time to pivot your business or career, you first:

   A. Take a step back and contemplate your options, then follow your intuition on which option to take
   B. Call a friend and brainstorm some options
   C. List out your top three options and choose one that feels the most fun
   D. Research some new options online, perhaps talk to a few mentors and see what approach they would suggest, and then sift through the options and see which one is best suited to move the career/business forward
   E. Reach out to trusted advisors for support and study what other people in similar industries have done, then make a decision that feels like it serves you and your community in the best way possible

4. You signed a contract and immediately realize you made a mistake. You want to keep your word, but you know that moving forward won't work. What do you do?

   A. You stay true to your intuition and do whatever it takes to negotiate a win/win and are willing to walk away from the money so you can stay true to what is aligned for you

B. Because you know that there is a better solution available, you call the company and ask them for your money back because it's within the contract cancellation period.

C. You ask yourself some questions to reflect on your options, and then you go with the one that feels best to you. You ponder what made you say yes to something that wasn't ideal so you can learn and not repeat the mistake again

D. You call your lawyer and ask them what your options are in a situation like this

E. You call a friend to console you because you're scared that you've made a mistake and start beating yourself up about it

5. A natural disaster has just occurred in an area where you do business. It affects your employees and their families. Even if your insurance company doesn't carry liability insurance that covers such matters, you decide to:

   A. Pray for everyone's welfare and let them know that they are in your prayers

   B. Call all your employees and family members and ask how you can help them

   C. Reach out to other business owners and get ideas of how they are helping their employees so you can determine the best option to take

   D. Speak to a local organization on the ground and have them reach your employees and provide key assistance to them

   E. Create a special package of resources (time off/extra pay for overtime) so they know not to worry about being taken care of—even if this means hiring extra personnel to cover for them while they are gone

6. A colleague's child gets very ill suddenly, to the point that it affects their ability to do their work and their schedule. Your reaction is to:

   A. Run a prayer vigil to provide energetic and nurturing support for the family and the company's employees

   B. Create a fundraiser to see how you can support their family as they navigate this ordeal

   C. Donate your own money to them anonymously

   D. Try your best to cheer the person up and boost their morale

   E. Ask how you can help and figure out a way to delegate or take some of their workload off of their plate

7. In general, your approach to navigating important steps in your life has been to:

    A. Go with what feels like the best course of action

    B. Focus on the most efficient way to create the biggest impact

    C. Research options about the best practices or solutions for your particular situation

    D. Look for the most inspiring and fun path to take, even if people think you're crazy

    E. Imagine what you can do to bring people together for the greatest outcome

8. You feel you want to get more joy and meaning out of your career. As a next step, you decide to:

    A. Shift careers entirely and follow your passion, even if that initially means a pay cut

    B. Identify what you want to do next and go for it 100% without hesitation, excited for what's to come

    C. Hire a career counselor and do extensive research on your next best options, including interviewing people in the various fields you're researching

    D. Quit and take some time off to see the world and enjoy your hobbies, as long as your savings account permits

    E. Join some transition groups and get support from a like-minded group of people so you're not trying to make the shift all by yourself

9. What would you say are your greatest strengths?

    A. I live for transformation; I follow my intuition and let it lead my life and decisions no matter what.

    B. Be bold or go home; I am a go-getter, and once I decide what I want I go for it full force.

    C. There is always an efficient solution; I rely on data and solid information to make my decisions, trusting that it can show me the best path forward.

    D. Life is an adventure; I follow my passions and take risks even when other people think they know what's best for me.

    E. We are all in this together; I know how to connect to other people and to build communities of supportive and like-minded people.

How to find your results: Tabulate how many of your responses correspond with each letter; the letter with the most responses is your Soulfluent® Leadership Archetype.

RESULTS:

1.   6.

2.   7.

3.   8.

4.   9.

5.

A= Mystic   **B**= Visionary   **C**= Strategist   **D**= Explorer   **E**= Divine Feminine

Keep in mind

Please remember that you are a culmination of ALL the Archetypes—as are those around you. More importantly, your team members, coworkers, colleagues, investors, collaborators each have their OWN primary Soulfluent® Leadership Archetype that informs not only how they run their business, but how they work best, how they manifest, and all their gifts and pitfalls.

As you go through the book, it may be tempting to focus only on your primary Archetype. However, you are invited to become familiar with each of the Archetypes, which will help you understand, relate to, and positively influence those who matter most, starting with the people you work with and for. When you can relate to them better, you can co-create more effectively and with greater efficiency, innovation, and harmony.

Give yourself space to let this information sink in. While it can be tempting to dismiss some of this content, especially the parts that are uncomfortable, give this material a chance to work its magic. Because the sheer volume of detail can be a little overwhelming, take things slow; go in stages. Start with your Archetype and then share the quiz with your inner circle and ask them to identify their primary Archetype as well. The team-building section is especially illuminating and can be highly transformative to share with those you work with. It can be a great conversation starter as well as a relationship and trust builder.

Above all, take your time, have fun with the material, and trust the process. If you work it, it will work for you—guaranteed. The key is to live, breathe life and trust into your Archetype, and let it guide you and inform your business decisions and how you show up for your mission, vision, and the greater good.

You've got this! I can't wait to hear what you create. Please email me at priscilla@priscillastephan.com and share how this work has helped you and your team.

Notes

Notes

Notes

Notes

Notes

About the Author
Priscilla Stephan

When entrepreneurs want to grow their business without working harder or burning out, they work with Priscilla Stephan, Intuitive Business Strategist and creator of the Soulfluent® Leadership Archetypes.

Through a powerful combination of practical business strategy together with soul guidance in the Akashic Records, she excels at helping people identify their zones of genius, step into powerful leadership, and live their purpose profitably.

Originally from Brazil, Priscilla is now based out of Northern California, where she works with leaders from a wide range of industries who have one thing in common: the desire to create a global impact and live a life of purpose without sacrificing their time, relationships, or well-being.

Over the last decade, she has helped hundreds of women grow sustainable, world-changing businesses and to develop their spiritual core by leading from their soul's wisdom.

Priscilla's been committed to serving the greater good since her early career days working as a Program Officer at the World Wildlife Fund® in Washington, DC, where she worked with high-level government leaders for a decade, creating new environmental policies that would support a sustainable planet. She holds a Master's Degree in International Relations from Columbia University, a Bachelor's degree from NYU, and speaks four languages: English, Portuguese, and conversational Spanish and French. On weekends you'll find her hiking with her husband Alex, watching soccer, eating decadent chocolate truffles, and playing with her cats Annabelle and Bodhi and her maltipoo Lily.

What's next?

Are you an established, mission-driven entrepreneur ready to take your business to the next level?

My private coaching programs provide one-on-one support as you sustainably grow your company to new heights. Ideal candidates are:

- Self-starters with an established mission-driven business
- Open to a spiritual and practical approach
- Ready to remove bottlenecks in their business, gain freedom, and honor themselves by working in a way that feels natural and true.

If this is you, apply here: www.priscillastephan.com/letstalk.

Please know that my private coaching is a premium investment and space is limited, as I can only accept a set number of clients each year.

Alternatively, if you want to learn more about your Soulfluent® Leadership Archetype and my other programs, visit my website: www.priscillastephan.com or contact me at: priscilla@priscillastephan.com. I look forward to hearing from you!

For Organizations and Teams:

Would you like to bring the Soulfluent® Leadership Archetypes work to your organization to strengthen the potency of your teams and leaders?

If so, email: priscilla@priscillastephan to discuss further or book a call here: www.priscillastephan.com/letstalk

Acknowledgments

The well-known adage that it takes a village to write a book, even a business guide, is very much true.

While this book was initially sparked by a conversation with my colleague Andrya Allen and then the concept reinforced while talking to my business coach Angella Johnson, it's taken collaboration with a lot of good souls to make it the high-quality product you have in your hands now.

First, to my colleagues who generously proofread the introduction and their specific Soulfluent® Leadership Archetypes and gave me their kind and honest feedback to make this guide even better. These include: Jacqueline Boone, Carolynn Bottino, Diana Dorrell, Angella Johnson, Bettina Laux, Rebecca Massoud, Debora McLaughlin, Heather Rangel, Nicole Richardson, Morgan Sheets, Annie Sisson, and Lisa Wechtenhiser.

Second, to the over thirty women and men who went through the Soulfluent® Leadership Roundtables in 2020 and provided me with real-life feedback on the power of this work and how it can positively affect their businesses. I am so grateful for your faith in me and in this work.

Third, to the incredible women and men, including those showcased in this guide, who show up and lead authentically through their Archetype every day with grace, courage, and transparency. I applaud you for your resilience and strength, and I am grateful for the light you bring to the world.

And to my dear family and friends who cheered me on, particularly on the days when it felt like this project would never end. A special thanks to my loving husband Alex Turner, my mama, my friends Alexis Logan, Jill Fleming, Candy Hozza, and especially Lindsay Pera, who encouraged me to turn this content into a published book.

Last but not least to my team: Carolyn Sheltraw, who designed the interior of this book; Jessica Lynn, who created the cover design; Madeleine Eno, who performed the monumental job of developmental editing to turn a channeled body of work into tangible material; Jennifer Williams, for copyediting and proofreading; Shanda Trofe, Sandi Masori, and Caroline Allen, who helped me navigate the choppy technical waters of self-publishing; and my business attorney, Robin Kravitz.

For anyone I may have forgotten in this section, please know the omission was not intentional and that I deeply appreciate your encouragement and support—truly.

I am humbled to be the channel through which the Higher energy of the Soulfluent® Leadership Archetypes body of work was birthed into the world and grateful it will continue to touch many lives as a result.

May you enjoy this guide in good health, and may it bring you joy and a sense of wonder and ever-increasing magic in your life.

–Priscilla

www.ingramcontent.com/pod-product-compliance
Lightning Source LLC
Chambersburg PA
CBHW052341210326
41597CB00037B/6213